LOVE AND PROFIT

LOVE AND PROFIT
THE ART OF CARING LEADERSHIP

JAMES A. AUTRY

AVON BOOKS ▲ NEW YORK

AVON BOOKS
A division of
The Hearst Corporation
1350 Avenue of the Americas
New York, New York 10019

The William Morrow and Company edition contains the following Library of Congress
Cataloging in Publication Data:

Autry, James A.
  Love and profit : the art of caring leadership / James A. Autry
     p.   cm.
  1. Job enrichment.   2. Caring.   3. Interpersonal relations.
4. Organizational change.   I. Title.
HF5549.5.J616A965   1990
650.1—dc20   90-34165
                                                               CIP

First Avon Books Trade Printing: September 1992

OPM   10   9   8   7   6   5   4   3

For Sally and Ronald, Jim and Julie, Rick and Lyn . . .

Acknowledgments

Were I to thank everyone who contributed in some way to
this book, I would have to thank all those who contributed in
some way to my development as a manager—even those who
did it by demonstrating bad management.

But that seems a bit much, so I'll acknowledge those who
had a positive role, whether they knew it or not, in leading
me to write a book about management.

I start with Bob Burnett, friend, leader, manager, mentor,
and good example-setter of the first order. Bob was the first
man I ever heard use the word *love* as an attribute of someone
in business. It was more than twenty years ago, in a speech
to managers, on the subject of self-renewal. The reaction in
the room was palpable, almost one of shock, and at the time
I marveled at how gutsy Bob was in just saying the word.
Apparently it did not hurt his career. He became president
and chief executive officer of Meredith Corporation, and now
is chairman of the board.

I also want to thank Meredith's present CEO, Jack Rehm,
for his friendship and support, even when he does not agree
with me. His honesty and straightforwardness, not to mention

his acceptance of individuality—even eccentricity—continue to make Meredith one of the most human of companies.

There are many other colleagues from whom I have learned a great deal, and there are many who teach me still, but space will not permit me to list them all.

There also are colleagues no longer living who made my work and my life fuller and more enjoyable. Among those I remember especially Red Seney, Wayne Miller, and Bill McReynolds.

Several friends have been consistently encouraging about this book, from its early stages through the final manuscript. A special thanks, though, to Betty Sue Flowers and Michelle Urry.

I am indebted to the Columbus Day Celebrants, who know who they are but who may not realize how important they have been to this book.

Thanks also to others whose comments or insights were helpful along the way: Marilyn Ferguson, David Jordan, Dorothy Kalins, Barry Flint, Hyla Cass, Joel Edelman.

And I want to express publicly my appreciation to Myrna Blyth for opening some important doors.

I would be remiss in not thanking John Naisbitt and Patricia Aburdene for their enthusiastic response to my "business poetry" and for their recommendation that I contact their agent.

Which brings me to Rafe Sagalyn, John and Pat's agent (and now mine). Not only did Rafe not flinch at the thought of trying to sell a business book with poetry in it, but he actually embraced the notion with enthusiasm.

The person who responded to Rafe's enthusiasm was Adrian Zackheim, an editor willing to take a chance on the unconventional. Thank you, Adrian. I hope this book will join your string of successes.

These acknowledgments are evidence that this book is no different from most others in that it cannot be credited to me, the author, alone. If the by-line was to be shared, however, it should be shared with my wife, Sally. She has worked with me every minute, reacting, editing, and critiquing—plus contributing ideas, insights, and observations from her own experience.

Thank you also, Sally, for your unending patience and support during all those hours I spent alone with the word processor. You made this book important to you only because you knew it was important to me.

... ...

Thank you also, Sally, for your unending patience and ...

Contents

LOVE AND PROFIT

Introduction

First, a few straightforward statements about some of my beliefs regarding work and management:

1. Work can provide the opportunity for spiritual and personal, as well as financial, growth. If it doesn't, then we're wasting far too much of our lives on it.

2. The workplace is rapidly becoming a new neighborhood, and American businesspeople are helping make it happen.

3. Good management is largely a matter of love. Or if you're uncomfortable with that word, call it caring, because proper management involves caring for people, not manipulating them.

Those who have read this far and think what I've said is too crazy for business should stop reading now.

For the others, I want to offer in this book a very personal perspective on management, on creating a climate for creative productivity. These observations are based on my twenty-eight years of management, many of which were spent doing the wrong things because I didn't know what I know now (a familiar refrain from most of us in the over-fifty crowd).

So just what do I know now that I didn't know then?

The answer starts this way: There are two kinds of managers: 1. Those who practice management as a trainable skill with all sorts of technical and administrative aspects that, when pursued properly, serve to direct people in performing for the company's best interest; and 2. Those who approach management as a calling, a life engagement that, if done properly, combines technical and administrative skills with vision, compassion, honesty, and trust to create an environment in which people can grow personally, can feel fulfilled, can contribute to a common good, and can share in the psychic and financial rewards of a job well done.

The thoughts expressed here concern the accelerating and widespread need for more managers of the second approach.

In case you haven't noticed, we're in the midst of a turning point in the history of business. The last chapter on management by fear is about to be written. I think it's time to wake up out there in the halls of traditional old-line management, time to wake up in the business-school classrooms. It's time to fully accept what's going on in the society, in the workplace, in the management-training pool, in the labor unions. It's time to reexamine the old notions about power.

Let's start by admitting that there has been a lot of mythology about individual freedom. Not that we don't philosophically believe in it. But organizationally we've had a lot of trouble making it work.

This country was founded on respect for individual rights and freedom of choice, but our institutions have rarely organized themselves to practice the pluralism they preach. Government, education, business, and even the church, for the most part have been governed—managed—by traditional hierarchies of increasing levels of authority. In other words, the old military squad-platoon-company-battalion model. In that model, you may choose to call the driving force whatever you like, but it boils down to authority and fear of authority.

But now, in business, management by fear is coming to an end. While there are still levels of authority, concepts of *power* are changing rapidly.

A paradox of management is that too many managers take themselves too seriously while too few take management seriously enough.

Management is not simply a skill or a technique or a profession. Management is not simply something you do as a part of your climb up the career ladder. Management, approached properly and with the attitude required for excellence, is a *calling*.

Despite the mechanisms of promotion, you don't become a manager because someone appointed you to be one. Hanging a title after your name and putting you at the top of the organization chart doesn't make you a manager. That only makes you a boss.

Management is, in fact, a sacred trust in which the well-being of other people is put in your care during most of their waking hours. It is a trust placed upon you first by those who put you in the job, but more important than that, it is a trust placed upon you after you get the job *by those whom you are to manage.*

The idea of management as a sacred trust finds its proof in the functions that always have attended positions of leadership and caring, and while this kind of management does not concern itself with old-line power, managing people is nonetheless an expression of power.

So remember this: A promotion to manager can give *authority*, but not power. It is the people you are to manage who will give you power; by their actions and response, they will bestow power on you, but only if they trust you to use it well.

So management is a matter of being "in relationship." This is one of the most overlooked and misunderstood principles in management.

Wherever did we get the notion that, in management, there is a reasonable and acceptable separation of the intellect and the spirit—that, in our work-world terms, the intellect controls the rational work life and the spirit is relegated to the soft stuff of romance, family, and religion? Where did it come from, all this hiding of emotion, of the spirit, of passion, behind some cool mask of macho detachment? I wonder if it is that business is considered too important to be diluted by all those feelings, or is it that business is not considered important enough to deserve them? Either way is wrong.

Most managers, like most professional news journalists, choose to stand back and observe people and make commentary—abstract and aloof—rather than participating in the lives of people.

But the minute you hire someone, or become a manager, your life becomes inextricably intertwined with your employees. Try as you may, you cannot escape the responsibility. So to deal with it, you can be the traditional old-line manager, which for most people provides convenient places to hide, or you can really care about the people you work with.

Now wait.

I am not some sort of Leo Buscaglia gone mad in the corporate marketplace. I simply believe in a whole, integrated way of thinking about business and personal relationships. This way of thinking translated into management techniques will ensure not only the employees' growth, but the manager's as well, and out of this will come the business advantage that happens when people are creative, innovative, and productive.

And I am not talking about undisciplined and indulgent management. In fact, if you are looking for an easier way to manage business effectively, you've read too far. What I'm talking about is harder, much harder. The rewards will not come in feelings of self-importance, in power trips, in the trappings of status. Rather, the rewards will come in more enduring ways: higher productivity, higher morale, higher profits, better return on investment, and greater opportunity for employees and for managers.

And I don't believe there is a collection of tips or tricks or gimmicks with which you can manipulate people under the guise of motivating them.

We should not get all caught up in the latest pop-business wisdom as it changes year after year: participatory management, the a-b-c-d theories, the curse of short-term thinking, "job enrichment," the several-minute managers, the "lean and mean" operation, the new streamlined organizational structures.

Some of that stuff is good. Some of it can and does work, but none of it is as important as the concept of creating an environment for people, a caring environment that lets you manage business for personal growth as well as—and as a way to achieve—financial growth. No fad. No new structure. Just a way of thinking and being that liberates you from all the old straw-boss, "policeman" duties, and lets you focus on how to do more things better more often.

If there were simple rules for applying this philosophical

approach, I'd lay them out. Only problem is, they would soon change because people change, and this kind of management involves itself with staying ahead of those changes.

While there are no rules, I do offer five uncomplicated guidelines that may help:

1. Avoid in-box management. This widespread style is defined as sitting at your desk, monitoring the in-box, and waiting for someone to make a mistake so you'll have something to do. If you're in touch with your employees regularly, then the in-box will never surprise you and the "mistakes" will dwindle, both in number and in importance.

2. Care about yourself. The good manager begins by managing (and caring about) himself. As Charles Garfield, in his work with "peak performers," has said, "You don't go through life 'motivating' people; you *jumpstart* them." And you can't jumpstart anyone unless your own battery is charged.

3. Be honest. Honesty is the single most important attribute in a manager's relationship with employees and fellow workers. This gets tough when you have to make critical appraisals of an employee. But if you *really care* about helping that person, you must be able to say, "Jim, I care about you and about your work, and I have to tell you that you are not performing as well as you must to get the job done." You can offer to help, of course, but honesty and caring also involve setting standards and applying them equitably. That honesty extends to putting people on probation and—rarely, we hope—firing people. And even firing can be an act of caring, though you'll rarely be thanked for it. (Remember, I said this is not indulgent management. No matter how tough a manager may seem, dishonesty is weakness.)

4. Trust your employees. Most of our governmental and business organizations manage to make people feel distrusted.

5. If you don't care about people, get out of management before it's too late. I mean it. Save yourself a heart attack and save many other people a lot of daily grief. I know a manufacturer of farm equipment in Iowa who told me, "I always tell my supervisors, 'Those workers want to know how much you care before they care how much you know.' "

What I have set out to do in the following chapters, in prose and poetry, is to expand on these simple rules, to put them in context with what so many business people call "the real world" of management.

In addition, I hope to pull away some of the macho scab of business and get to the real life of it, the emotion of it. I hope to demonstrate not only how it *is* to be a good manager but how it *feels* to be a good manager—the joy, the pride, the pain, and the disappointment of a life fully engaged every day.

Do not expect anything here about systems and structures, because *management is not about systems and structures.*

Management is an art, an almost organic process. And because it is a process that cannot be fixed in time or measured precisely, no one can do it perfectly. We are all practicing.

But if we have the courage to keep refining our philosophies and our art toward the creation of a workplace of growth and caring, business will be the better for it.

LOVE AND PROFIT

"I slept and dreamt that life was Joy;
  and then I awoke and realized
  that life was Duty.
And then I went to work—and, lo
  and behold I discovered that
Duty can be Joy."

—Rabindranath Tagore
Indian spiritual leader

PART I

WORK AND LIFE: BUSINESS AND RELATIONSHIPS

Special Treatment

I THINK I started maturing as a manager when I discovered that one of the oldest principles of organizational management was hogwash. That principle is stated in many ways, but the military guys used to put it best: "Nobody gets special treatment around here."

How many times have you been exposed to—or used—that old management hiding place? In the military, they might also say, "If we do this for you, Lieutenant Autry, we'll have to do it for everyone."

I used to want to say, "No, sir, you could do it just for me."

What I realize now is that the professed aversion to special treatment was all delusion anyway; people in every organization, including the military, get special treatment all the time. Unfortunately, much of it has tilted toward "in" groups, such as West Pointers, or graduates of the right business school. That kind of "special treatment" is favoritism and discrimination.

But there's another kind of special treatment that, simply stated, is a manager's willingness to bend the rules to accommodate every person's specialness, and this special treatment is an increasingly important tool in the new workplace.

Some people do good work but are slow; some do fast work but are sloppy. Some are morning people; some do better in the afternoon. Some have children who cause schedule problems; some have elderly parents. Some need a lot of attention and affirmation; some want to be left alone to do their work. Some respond more to money, less to praise; some thrive on praise. Some are workaholics; some work only for the livelihood.

Then, of course, some are very bright; some are slow. Some have physical or mental disabilities; some are whole and strong. Some are men; some are women.

Who in the world could believe that all those special needs could be accommodated without some special treatment?

But it takes a lot of management courage to provide the special treatment. No one wants to catch the heat for doing special, sometimes unusual, things.

A few years ago, a very bright and productive salesperson in my group came to me with a special request. Her husband was being transferred about a hundred miles away from the city in which our offices were located. Because of child-care problems in the new location, she wanted to be allowed to remain on full-time employment but work at home two days a week, coming to the office only three days a week. She promised to keep up with her accounts and to remain as effective as ever.

I agreed to give it a try. There was resentment, most of which, surprisingly, came from other women on the staff. The personnel director didn't like it at all. "Bad precedent and outside policy." And my boss didn't like it very much, either, for the same reasons.

At this point, you think I'm about to glory in my vindication. Not true. It didn't work out. But it did not stop me from trying another outside-the-policy accommodation for a new mother who convinced her managers and me that she could do productive, high-quality work by mixing office and home time. She simply wanted to be with her first child, at home, longer than policy allowed. Her record was good. Her commitment to her work and to the company effort was unquestioned, and her work itself was of outstanding quality.

And in this case, the special treatment worked perfectly—for the company, for her, and, I trust, for the baby.

I've made exceptions to corporate rules to help get an employee's family through the nightmare of overwhelming financial and emotional distress. I've made similar exceptions for employees needing assistance to recover from substance abuse.

Our company has flex hours—a nice innovation, but even so, an individual employee may need to flex the hours a bit beyond the policy from time to time. My policy is that it's between the person and the supervisor, and the supervisors know that I generally choose the side of flexibility.

I've seen a company CEO arrange for a corporate contribution to a health-care facility, specifically to help a former employee whose family could not bear the financial burden of his terminal illness.

The road of special treatment is not without peril, and it makes day-to-day management much trickier and more time-consuming. You must consider the impact on the group, the legal risks, and the questions of equity and justice, in addition to the record and commitment of the person involved. Then, if at all possible, decide in favor of special treatment.

There will be the potshotters and detractors, the people who worry about precedent and control, who worry that the other employees will become resentful.

But there is only one answer to that: Trust the great majority of your employees to know that you are trying to do the right thing and that their time will come.

When someone complains, just say, "Everyone gets special treatment around here."

THREADS

Sometimes you just connect,
like that,
no big thing maybe
but something beyond the usual business stuff.
It comes and goes quickly
so you have to pay attention,
a change in the eyes
when you ask about the family,
a pain flickering behind the statistics
about a boy and a girl in school,
or about seeing them every other Sunday.
An older guy talks about his bride,
a little affectation after twenty-five years.
A hot-eyed achiever laughs before you want him to.
Someone tells about his wife's job
or why she quit working to stay home.
An old joker needs another laugh on the way
to retirement.
A woman says she spends a lot of her salary
on an au pair
and a good one is hard to find
but worth it because there's nothing more important
than the baby.
Listen.
In every office
you hear the threads
of love and joy and fear and guilt,
the cries for celebration and reassurance,
and somehow you know that connecting those
    threads
is what you are supposed to do
and business takes care of itself.

In the Face of
Impossible Choices

MOST OF the management choices, or "decisions," we make are obvious. We may not like to admit it, but in fact our instinct is for the obvious and generally for what is officially "right." This is, of course, the safe and proven approach to management.

But consider the news story a few years ago of the old, experienced captain of a Lockheed 1011 jumbo jet who, after taking off from San Francisco, could not get the nose down. He tried everything within reason, even putting his feet against the control column and pushing with all the strength he and his co-pilot could muster. The nose continued upward toward a sure stall. The engines simply would not have enough power to keep the big plane climbing at such a steep angle.

Just at the point when other pilots might only have hoped for a miracle, the captain pulled back the throttles, reducing engine power. On the face of it, this was madness, an action so precisely opposite of accepted flying technique that 95 percent of all the pilots in the world would have judged it suicide. Who but a madman would reduce power in the face of a stall?

Everyone knows the result. The nose, responding to less

power for some reason, lowered, and did it quickly enough to avert a stall. The pilot was able to nurse the plane back to San Francisco, a major deficiency was discovered, all other L1011s were repaired, and, I'm sure, many lives were saved.

The captain explained, "When you try everything that's supposed to work and it doesn't work, the only thing left is what's not supposed to work."

Few management decisions have the potential of saving lives, but there are times when we should reexamine the definition of "saving lives." And there surely are times when we should ignore our instincts for the obvious.

Take for instance the situation in which an employee is stricken with cancer and seems destined to die. In my case, he was a department head, a longtime employee, a solid and savvy manager, and a pragmatist.

"Look, Jim," he said from his hospital bed, "I want to try to beat this thing, and the best way I can do it is to get back to work. I won't be able to travel as much, but I can do everything else."

He said he would have staff meetings in the hospital room, that he would keep up with the reading and correspondence. Then, when he left the hospital, he'd come to the office in a wheelchair until he could walk again.

The issues were clear. How could we let this man hang on to the illusion that he could really do the job? How could we expect the other employees to accommodate his deficiencies? How could we tolerate the inevitable drop in productivity? And what about the impact on morale?

I had seen similar situations: Within a few months, the guilt sets in. The employees are uncomfortable with a dying person in their midst. They wonder why they should be healthy and he should be dying, but that is not what they say to themselves. They say, "Why does the company put up with this? Why don't they put him on disability leave or something?"

As in the decision to fire someone, sooner or later the well-being of the group should outweigh the well-being of the individual. But there's a big difference: In a firing, the person has another chance. There's always another possible job.

So, ignoring the precepts of consultative management by consulting with no one, I said, "Sure. You can do a better job in the hospital than most people can in an office anyhow."

He did as he said he would. But productivity did not drop. The other employees did make up for his deficiencies. And he worked until just a few weeks before he died.

Yes, there was the guilt. There were complaints. And morale did drop. But maybe there's a difference between low morale and the daily reminder that we are all dying, only by different degrees. If that's true, then who is to say it is inappropriate at the office to be brought face-to-face with our mortality?

Perhaps the other decision, the disability option, the officially accepted thing to do, would have been right. Maybe we could have avoided the gloom of the death cloud hanging for months in his department. We could have promoted someone else to the department-head job, had a celebration coffee, shaken our heads appropriately about the fate of our old friend, called and written cards, stopped by his house on the weekend, and gone about our business. Full throttle.

But we have to be beyond that. If we can't share the coming of death in the workplace, how in the world can we share life except in the most obvious and superficial of ways?

SENEY'S GONE

(In memory of Noel "Red" Seney, who taught me much)

With a stylistic nod to Donald Justice

There will be no more fun at the office.
Seney has died,
taking all his foolishness with him.
What will happen on a spring afternoon
when there is no Seney to lure us to the park
with a football, Frisbees, and a case of beer?
Will productivity rise
now that there is no silliness
to get in its way?

There will be no more fun at the office.
Seney has died,
taking all his foolishness with him.
How will we bear those meetings
to which Seney brought the only life,
a show-and-tell of some sort,
a joke perhaps or,
oh yes, a limerick
about ladies or men from places
that rhymed with an anatomic appendage?

It is easy to imagine Seney,
wherever he is,
still smoking and full of coffee,
organizing whatever parties they have there,
bringing angelic or demonic exuberance
to every new chorus
of "Chinamen never eat chili."

But there will be no more fun at the office.
Seney has died,
taking all his foolishness with him.
Where will we find the smiles
when things are late

and they're on our butts about the overtime,
when there's no way to get it all done
but we know we will
because we always do?
Where will we find the smiles?

WHAT TO KNOW ABOUT HANGING ON

I

Why do they keep on working,
the ones who should take everything,
the disability time,
the vacation,
the wink-and-look-the-other-way extras
they could get at a time like this?
Why don't they head for the fishing hole
they always talked about,
or the mountains,
or that spot far away from the cold,
the one they promised to send pictures
for us to hang in the garage
above our snow shovels?
Why do they make up excuses
to come in on time every morning
and return phone calls
and answer correspondence
and talk about next year's sales goals
and the plan
and the earnings
and the stock price
and the chances of a takeover—
everything as ordinary as always?

II

We used to say,
as they did,
if it happened to us
we would kiss the job good-bye
and pack every remaining minute
with people we love
and things we love to do.
Through all those years
it did not occur to us

that what we really love to do
is the work—
never mind the job
with all its trappings,
those things we have to do
so we can do the work,
and never mind that we talked about
loving the company
when we really meant
loving the people.

But now, watching someone hang on,
I long to say the words we feel
but never say,
about how hard it is to show
the love of what we do together,
until we face the certainty
that it is about to end.

THE MEMO

It looked like any other memo,
corporate proper and neat,
with "to" and "from" and "cc" in order,
with margins straight
and text centered.
It came through inter-office mail
and appeared on our desks
just like any other memo.
It was the subject,
"Three of the greatest lies,"
that caught our eyes and made us read,

    1. You can eat anything with false teeth.
    2. I've never lied to you.
    3. We think we got it all.

Then it talked of CAT scans
and something called a
squamous-cell lung carcinoma,
strange words to find in our in-boxes.

Of course, it was not the first memo
about a change in plans,
nor was it even the first memo about fear.
But we want action memos,
you see,
we want memos
that leave us with something to do.
And this was a memo
about waiting.

Management from the Roots

A POPULAR management technique of the past few years, popular to write about if not to do, is "Management by Walking About," or MBWA.

I've always had a little trouble with that one, because it seems to me that you ought to know why you're walking about. Is it to let the people know you're there? If you have to resort to some gimmick to let them know you're there, you aren't there enough.

Is it to stay in touch? If you think walking about and pausing at the water fountain or eating occasionally in the company cafeteria will keep you in touch, you're out of touch.

Is it to learn something? What do you think you'll learn from an employee who probably is shocked out of his skull that the boss just walked in unannounced?

Perhaps I'm too negative about what surely has proved itself for some managers, so let me offer some additional ways of thinking about yourself and of communicating with your people.

Management is a part of life, and life is largely a matter of paying attention. Listen and act on what you hear. Be attentive to personal needs and accomplishments as well as professional ones. Know when someone's teenager wins a scholarship and who won a golf or bowling tournament. Watch the company newsletter for birthdays and wedding anniversaries and birth announcements and service anniversaries and notices of people in the hospital or of deaths in the family of an employee. Then write a personal note.

And life is enriched by staying in touch with your own story. Think of your roots. Not just your family and geographical roots, but your management roots. Think about where you came from and how you got to where you are now.

I know very few managers who did not work their way up from the employee ranks, who did not suffer frustrations with an insensitive bureaucracy or a brutal boss at one time or another. Yet most seem to want to put all that behind them now that they are the management establishment. They want to believe that the employees don't understand the problems at the top.

Nonsense. These same managers understood a great deal more than their bosses gave them credit for years ago, but now they put on their management masks and cannot see or hear what their employees understand about "the big picture."

So the key is not walking about, it's opening up and letting go of the management mentality. It's paying attention and staying in touch. It's being brave enough to tell your employees you don't know everything and need their advice.

I regularly have coffees with small groups of randomly selected employees. I tell them my own goals for the magazine group. I tell them my management problems. I frequently ask, "What do you think we should do?" or say, "Tell me how your job is affected by these problems."

At budget meetings, I often say, "If the roles were reversed and I were submitting this budget to you, what would you ask me? Where would you tell me to cut it? Or would you?"

Remember, in your worker days you knew your job better

than your boss did, and you got where you are today not *despite* your roots as a worker in the ranks but *because* of them.

So walk about when it seems the right thing to do, but also consider Management from the Roots.

MFTR.

EDUCATED FOOL

My grandmother used to talk about educated fools,
  All they do is sit
  at a desk,
  never do any work.
and I dreamed about how easy that would be,
sitting at a desk
instead of sweating in the sun and dirt,
instead of chopping cotton
or picking up potatoes or pulling weeds,
instead of fighting flies and sting worms
and wasps and sometimes a snake.
"Educated fool" didn't sound so bad,
all desks and telephones and secretaries,
eating in some air-cooled café
instead of trying to find a dark spot
of tree shade on the edge of a field,
with a sausage and biscuit and a jug of tea,
nobody to talk to but a mule or dog.

You know what comes next, of course.
You know I'm writing this at my desk,
on a Thursday,
and day after tomorrow
I'll put on bib overalls,
the neighbors thinking what an affectation,
and pull weeds for the composter,
and dig a place for a late row of greens,
most of them going to seed
instead of in the pot,
and tell myself what the hell,
I just want to dig the dirt
and watch the stuff grow,
an educated fool at last.

Building Business Means Building Relationships

I KNOW a successful businessman who says, "The way to do business with people is to do business with *people*."

Business, like art and science, has been revealed and conceived through the intellect and imagination of people, and it develops or declines because of the intellect and imagination of people.

In fact, there is no business; there are only people. Business exists only *among* people and *for* people.

Seems simple enough, and it applies to every aspect of business, but not enough businesspeople seem to get it.

Reading the economic forecasts and the indicators and the ratios and the rates of this or that, someone from another planet might actually believe that there really are invisible hands at work in the marketplace.

It's easy to forget what the measurements are measuring. Every number—from productivity rates to salaries—is just a device contrived by people to measure the results of the enterprise of other people. For managers, the most important job is not measurement but motivation. And you can't motivate numbers.

My businessman friend knows that his business is better when his relationships are better, whether they are with customers, vendors, or employees. He knows that relationships are built on reaching people as people, not as digits.

He tells the truth. He says what he knows in his heart to be true, and people believe him because they *want* to believe him. He solves most problems by helping people find solutions. He understands the spirit of business, holding the belief that everyone in the same business shares a common bond and wants to have that bond reinforced, person to person.

There is no faster proof of his beliefs than in selling. Most sales managers have experienced how dramatically business can turn up or down when a different salesperson is assigned to an account. Often the only thing required to get more business is to assign a problem account to someone who knows how to find the common bonds.

No matter what anyone tells you, when you lose business, it's almost *always* a relationship problem. Good relationships and personal connections can come only when you abandon the patterned thinking and language of business. Most business language tries to communicate the intellectual technicalities of business, and is somewhat efficient in doing so, but this language has no place in the vocabulary of feelings and ideas that make up the spirit of business.

Peter Drucker has pointed out that "management always lives, works, and practices in and for an institution. And an institution is a human community held together by the bond that, next to the tie of family, is the most powerful human bond: the work bond."

I find no further justification necessary for a new emphasis on management that is caring and supportive, that views itself as a "helping profession."

It is in this frame of mind about management that you will find the personal connections that open a clearer path for the doing of business.

Removing the Manager Mask

A FEW years ago, I was to meet with a well-known and highly respected media executive with a large advertising agency. It was during an occasional West Coast visit that I had arranged to make sales calls with our branch-office salespeople.

"This guy's a toughie," said our salesman in the territory. "He was really pissed last year by a reproduction problem we had, and I'm afraid we didn't give him much satisfaction."

Clearly, our salesman expected the meeting to be confrontational, and he led me to believe that our lunch guest expected the same.

In questioning the salesman, I learned that his personal relationship with the angry adman was okay; their children were acquainted; they respected one another; and occasionally they socialized. This told me that our guest was unhappy with the company, not the person who represented the company —which probably is why we were still getting business from him. This told me also that he was willing to put value on the human aspects of business.

We met, made a little talk about the weather and my trip from the Midwest, then I said, "Jim, I know you feel we've mistreated you and your client. I understand that your job is to represent your client's best interest. Why don't you just tell me what we can do to make you and your client happy with us once again and we'll do it. I want us to be able to work together without any prejudice."

He was stunned and a bit suspicious, so I added, "There's no slow curve with a fast break; what you hear is what I mean. Name what you want. There's no deadline; call me anytime."

He relaxed.

Then I purposely did not talk about business again during the two-hour lunch. Instead, I told him that I had been anxious about our meeting, confessing a fear of confrontation that I found difficult to overcome. It was that chink in my armor that led him to talk about himself. We found we agreed on many matters of philosophy and business, including our feeling that love—of our peers, of our work, of our customers, of the results of our efforts—was the most important ingredient of business.

When we said good-bye, we hugged, a warm and solid expression of affection and respect. We've become close acquaintances, though we don't get together often. And he still complains if we don't treat him well, as he should.

Doing business with people means only that we recognize and accept our humanness. It means attention to the human things: illness, death, marriage, childbirth. It means notes, calls, and visits.

And it means the willingness to not hide your own humanness behind the manager mask.

THE LEADER

It was in the big paneled office,
on the sofa,
after a run at the Y,
that he said,
tears and sweat on his face,
"I've been such an asshole,"
then he bear-hugged me and said,
"You have to stay,
you're one of my people."
And I thought,
Okay if I can be this kind of businessman,
I'll be a businessman.

Then, somewhere along the way,
it got harder for him.
The skeptics, I think,
the loneliness.
He did not want to find any truth
in the old cliché
about isolation at the top,
but the gentle touch is more difficult
than the strong arm,
and a balancing act is more tiring
than you think.

But when I am patient
and look beyond the obvious,
it is still there,
something I am supposed to preserve.

I AM THAT MAN

(In memory of Wayne Miller)

James Dickey once put on a dead man's helmet,
a man just killed in battle,
and Dickey's head filled with the dead man's last
   thoughts.

That poem came to me in a dead man's office
as I was arranging my stuff,
making my place in his place.
He faced one way, I would face another.
He liked blank walls and overhead lights,
I like paintings and plants for my eye
wherever it wanders.
He was quick with aphorisms
like "Plan your work and work your plan,"
and he knew that hard work
overcomes guile every time.
He believed in ladies and gentlemen
and starting on time
and being frugal with an expense account
("Treat the company's money like your own.")
And he was always one man at home
and the same man on the job.

Times change, of course, but I wonder,
if I wear this office like that dead soldier's helmet,
will they call me quaint some day?
Will my insights become sayings
that everybody thinks they've heard too often?
Will my truths become anachronisms
while another person measures my corner office?
Will I settle into this part of my business journey
like a man who sees time gathering
on both sides of every day,
who believes that things don't change
but that we talk about them differently?

Will I feel something gentle someday,
something calm come into the office,
and will I look out the window
and see children throwing clods in the river
and a mother gathering dry milkweed pods,
and will I know that, later,
a man will see them in a vase
on a table in a room
where he will read the Twenty-third Psalm before
    dinner,
home at last?
And will I know that I am that man?

The Job and the Work

In HIS book *The Ascent of Man*, Jacob Bronowski, speaking of the history of humankind, said, "The personal commitment of a man to his skill, the intellectual commitment and emotional commitment working together as one, has made the ascent of man."

A good way to think about commitment is as dedication to the work a person has chosen to do. Not as dedication to a job.

The difference is not frivolous, because it goes to the heart of an employee's attitude about what he or she does.

What we set ourselves to do is not the same as holding a job.

When an employee (or a manager) says, "I do my job," chances are he is not very emotionally involved in the substance of what he does.

I frequently meet people who claim to love their jobs but mean that they love the style of it, not the substance. "I love being a sales rep" is not the same as, "I love selling."

"I love being a magazine writer" is not the same as "I love writing."

"I love being a manager (or a vice president or a department head)" is a far cry from "I love being able to get people to accomplish goals together."

Before you write this off as an artificial distinction, try a little survey. Ask people in your company what they would miss most about their work if they were to leave.

Unfortunately, a majority probably will describe the "job" stuff, the ancillary activities that surround the real work.

I have fired two separate people who, in their disappointment and grief, asked if the company might maintain certain things for them, like a car or a club membership.

Obviously, their focus had been on the trappings and not on the work.

These attitudes are understandable given the emphasis we place—in our society as well as in business—on the symbols of status and achievement. It often seems quite compelling as well as entirely reasonable to put a lot of time and effort into maintaining the rewards to the detriment of the reason we get the rewards.

I knew a manager who was able to convince himself that his duties as an officer of his country club were as deserving of his attention as his duties on the job for which he was given the country-club membership as a perk!

It will serve any manager well to watch out for the job-lover, then to help that person focus on the work. We've all let people fail by not keeping them focused through goal-setting and honest appraisals, both of which should be about the real work.

I've had to fire people who loved the job, but I don't believe I've ever fired anyone who loved the work.

THE MEANING OF RICH

When we said someone was rich,
we meant only one thing:
He never had to work another day in his life.
We did not know how much money it would take,
but as we entered the sweepstakes
and jingle contests
and shouted our quiz-show answers at the radio,
we figured sixty-four-thousand dollars would do just
   fine,
fifty dollars a week forever
and never work another day in our lives.

Money comes and goes,
and so does the meaning of rich,
but most of us retired before we learned
that nothing pays off
like having work to do.

The Case for Liberated Management

T HERE'S A lot of talk these days about leadership and how leadership is the true goal of the manager. Who could disagree that it would be nice if every manager could have extraordinary vision and charisma and could articulate that vision with such inspiration and clarity that the employees would achieve the objectives with great creativity, high morale, and superior productivity?

But all the current demands for "leadership" have become very intimidating for managers. For good reason. It is almost impossible to define leadership. It's kind of like art: You know it when you see it, which doesn't mean you can do it yourself.

It is better, I think, to turn down the pressure for leadership and concentrate on changing ordinary managers into good managers.

In fact, by removing a lot of the unrealistic and sometimes counterproductive expectations, we could establish a whole new kind of manager: the liberated manager.

First, let's liberate managers from "in-box management." We all know what that is: massive amounts of paperwork, most of it redundant and much of it a hindrance. Not only does it drive managers to bury themselves in paper, but it also makes them think their jobs are determined by what shows up in the In-box rather than out among the people.

Second, let's admit that the structures mean more in the annual report than they do on the job every day. Let's empower the manager and his people to impose their own "systems" and "flow charts" on a person-to-person basis without regard for what's written on paper.

Then, let's not expect all managers to have the gift of oratory. The articulation of vision can be as simple as the manager sharing his performance standards or personal goals, then relating those to the department's or group's goals.

Then, liberate managers from police work—monitoring office hours, lunch hours, dress codes, or coffee breaks, none of which has very much relationship to whether employees are productive.

The logical next step is to eliminate the notion of punishment. The whole concept of punishment as a tool of today's management is nonsense. No one should be docking pay or issuing official reprimands these days. There are more effective and enlightened ways to express dissatisfaction, primarily through appraisals and reward systems. A relatively lower merit increase, for instance, is not punitive; it becomes the tangible expression of an appraisal and is accompanied by the expectation that there are positive ways to improve it next time.

This leads, then, to liberating the managers from ever being in conflict with their own best human values.

So what does all this liberation amount to?

To a better workplace. To managers who engage the job fully every day, actively, positively, without spending the day at the desk, waiting for someone to screw up so they'll have something to do. To managers who understand that they succeed, both personally and professionally, as their people succeed. To managers who realize that *the employees really want to help the manager succeed*, one of the key understandings of good management.

When this happens, the managers no longer evaluate themselves by the old measurements of success, which is the most liberating thing of all.

And, say, if all this is beginning to make liberated management sound like leadership, then maybe leadership doesn't have to be so intimidating after all.

Sexual Harassment

I T'S ALL very well to talk about love and caring in the workplace, but now let's talk about sexual harassment.

Recently, I met with a young saleswoman, a feminist, whom I had hired and to whom I had been something of a mentor. It had been a while since we'd seen one another, so she gave me a warm and exuberant hug. It was important and appropriate. She initiated it, and I'm sure she thought nothing of it. But why? Why was it appropriate? I can name fifty other people with whom I have an equal relationship but with whom the hug would *not* have been appropriate. Why did she think nothing of it? Surely, she can name fifty men with whom she has worked but whom she would not have hugged. What was the difference?

She might have her own answer, but I know mine: The difference has to do with power and motive. Sexism and sexual harassment are *always* about power, not about affection and caring. Sexism and sexual harassment are *always* one-sided, never mutual.

And I know this: Employees, including managers, must care for one another, and the frequently intertwined nature of our personal/professional relationships makes rules impossible, except those clearly established by law.

I know this too: Somehow we *must* accept and tolerate appropriate expressions of caring, of support, and of affection in a workplace that now accepts many more of those expressions partly *because* so many women have come into business. It is ironic that I now find myself, more often than not, hugging men and then, because of uncertainty or the fear of being misunderstood, shaking hands with women.

If anything is clear, it is that men and women see sexual harassment differently. *The Wall Street Journal* reported a piece of research that showed that men and women generally agreed on what constitutes sexual harassment, but they did not agree on how women should respond. Forty-six percent of the men said that women should be flattered; only 5 percent of the women agreed.

It is difficult for many men to separate women's desire to be attractive and to express a sexual identity from their desire also to maintain a sexual privacy and separateness that is inviolable by words, looks, or gestures.

And the difficulty does not seem limited to men my age, men who came of age in the fifties. Indeed, I have had to deal firmly with sexual-harassment cases, and the offenders have been both younger and older.

In one instance, a sensitive and intelligent young man seemed simply to feel that his use of suggestive language and sexual innuendo were signs that he was in the "boys club" of management. Unfortunately for him, he lost his management position altogether.

In another case, a man and a woman had worked together for years. They had done many projects together, worked many overtime hours together, and had developed a personal familiarity and sense of partnership. But the man began to misread the affection. Worse, he would not believe that his longtime partner did not want a sexual relationship.

After he persisted despite a warning and his promise to back off, I had no choice but to remove him from the job.

Both of these cases ended sadly. Some might say the men

got their just punishment. Perhaps. But these cases were not about "bad" men or "indecent" men. They were about an inability or an unwillingness to accept the full equality of women in the workplace, which means they were about the need to express power through sex.

I admit that given the current legal climate, it would be safer to avoid expressing affection of any sort on the job. I admit too that an expression of caring affection for a fellow worker runs the risk of looking like an expression of sexual affection. But I believe strongly that those expressions are very different—and the difference is no big mystery.

Motive and mutuality are the keys to appropriateness, so despite the complexities, sexual harassment is not all that hard to identify, within ourselves or other people. I can recognize it when I see it. And so can you.

What's All This About Long Hours?

WE'RE ALWAYS reading in *The Wall Street Journal* or one of the business magazines a profile of some CEO who works ninety-hour weeks and who keeps up with every detail—and, of course, whose company is doing just dandy by all the right measurements.

We never seem to read about the CEO who works ninety-hour weeks and who keeps up with every detail and whose company is on the ropes. Nonetheless, those CEOs exist probably in about the same proportion as the ones who get profiled.

There are also CEOs who put in fewer hours, delegate more, and aren't preoccupied with the details, and whose companies are in great shape.

So what's my point?

Only that our business culture is preoccupied with what has become defined as "work habits."

Good work habits, by conventional definition, must include "getting to work on time" and the willingness to put in long hours, including weekend work.

I know a manager who truly believes that an employee's value is related to after-hours and weekend work. In fact, this guy doesn't quite trust the worker who gets the work done without spending at least a part of every weekend in the office, almost as if the job is not a full-time job if it doesn't require more than full time to do it.

Unfortunately for the work addicts in my group, I am not impressed by the worker who consistently puts in night and weekend hours to get the job done. I immediately begin to think something's wrong, either with the way the job is structured or the way it's being done.

Which is not to say that good professional work does not often require more time than a forty-hour week provides. But spare me what I call the balloon job, which will keep rising in time demand as long as someone keeps pumping hot air into it.

If we managers are true to what we claim, that we evaluate work and appraise performance based on results, then we shouldn't be concerned about work habits beyond two considerations: 1. The results are not as good as they should be, indicating that more diligence and time devoted to the job could help; and 2. The employee so abuses office hours and other work-habit expectations that it has a negative impact on department or group morale.

It probably comes as no surprise that the best performers *usually* are the ones who exhibit good work habits. But not always, particularly in some of the more creative disciplines.

Nonetheless, I never appraise work habits. Some managers enjoy the comfort of concentrating on work habits rather than on the work itself, because it is so much easier than real management—but I don't. Furthermore, the vast majority of employees never abuse the generally tolerant environment we've created.

W. L. Gore, the often-quoted executive, once said that "productivity comes from commitment not from authority." And commitment doesn't come from keeping up with the attendance record, nor is it measured by hours worked per week.

The best managers I know try to figure out why the work-addicted employees can't get the job done in a reasonable work week, thus leaving time for family, friends, hobbies, and other habits of a balanced life, which, in turn, will assure a longer, more productive work life.

And the best managers I know try to achieve that balance in their own lives as well—and for the same long-term reasons.

So the next time you read one of those profiles on a ninety-hours-a-week CEO, check to see if you have any of his company's stock. Then—unless you know something that will bolster the company when the CEO has a heart attack or a case of nervous exhaustion—sell.

BUSINESS IS BAD, I

How do you know when you've gone too far?
Maybe it's when someone asks,
"How are you?"
And you tell them how business is.
Maybe it's when business is bad
and it feels like a death in the family,
and you wonder how anybody can be happy,
the way you feel when you're on the way to a
    funeral
and find yourself wondering
why all those other people in the airport
are laughing and smiling as if no one had died.
Don't they know, don't they know?
Business is bad.

Maybe it's when you find yourself angry
in the midst of another, yet another,
birthday coffee or promotion party,
or when someone asks you to join a baseball pool
or attend a fund-raising lunch,
or stop for an after-work drink
with the such-and-such department,
which is celebrating
another of those productivity milestones
we invent so we'll have something to celebrate.
"How do they have time for this crap?"
you ask yourself.
Don't they know, don't they know?
Business is bad.

BUSINESS IS BAD, II

He did not look well,
the paunch of too many receptions and dinners
at too many conferences
in too many hotels.
(Sometimes it's smiling too much
I think
and saying the same thing
over and over again,
a kind of social fatigue.)
And here he was,
eating and drinking,
this time with friends,
—never mind that we all work together,
that we talk about those same things—
in the home of another friend,
so I asked, "How are you doing?"
with an emphasis on the you.
And he shook his head
and frowned and tucked his chin
and swallowed like someone
whose mouth is dry
and said,
"That last profit forecast was rotten,
really a killer."

Down-to-Earth Talk About Hype

On a college campus recently, an intense business-school student asked the question I'm sure he has asked every guest lecturer: "Do you have any advice for succeeding in business?"

So I gave him the guidelines: "Be smart, work harder than you thought you could or than anyone expects you to, take your work seriously but don't take yourself so seriously, don't get caught up in the glitz of business, and don't *ever* believe your own hype."

It was not an answer the student wanted to hear, and I suspect the professor was not happy with it either. The past decade or so has seen the emergence of businessman (and I mean "man") as national hero, businessman as celebrity. With all the press given to the giant takeover deals, business has taken on the aura of show business. It's as if all a big player has to do is make a move on a large corporation, and a star is born. Ten years ago, no one could spell or pronounce "arbitrageur," but until the recent Wall Street debacles, half of the business students in the country wanted to be one.

Lee Iacocca became Chrysler's major ad campaign, and as a result was almost drafted to run for president of the country.

Not many average citizens can name Farley Industries' products, but they sure know what Bill Farley looks like—and he *did* make a small run for the presidency.

There never has been as much public attention to business as in the past several years, so here was this student, with the glamorous world of business awaiting him, and there I was, dishing out this old-fashioned advice like "work hard" and "take your work seriously." I must have seemed like someone from another world.

But I have news for that student, and his professor, and all the business students in America, and all the upwardly striving managers everywhere: Real management is not glamorous, is not glitzy, is not the road to celebrity. Good managers think of their people first, then themselves.

One observation seems to emerge: The effective managers understand the place of promotion and public relations; they know how to make it work for their businesses. In fact, they realize that everything that could be called hype is a tool in the marketplace and not a commentary on how they really live their lives or do their business.

And there is a corollary observation: Effective managers really do take their work very seriously, but really do not take themselves so seriously.

Good managers know that sometimes they will get attention, in the company, in the press, in the community, in their industry. They may consciously seek attention, and they may enjoy the attention, but down deep they never forget that celebrity is a tempting trap, that the attention given them should always be a way of furthering the goals of their business, and that any hype surrounding them is just another tool of management.

One other thing they never kid themselves about: The half-life of hype is very short indeed, and no amount of hype will make up for incompetence, laziness, or bad products.

Leave the Ambition at the Door, Please

"**M**AKE SOMETHING of yourself!" all the books said. And, believing the books, our parents said the same thing. Of course, no one ever said what to make of ourselves. Just something.

The implication, we all came to understand, was that we were to try to get to the top, wherever that was, and in so doing one of the things we were probably to make of ourselves was a hard-ass manager. And if we got to the top, we were conditioned to find it lonely there, not because the awesome responsibilities were too great for the subordinates to understand, but because we had stepped on so many of them on the way up.

Written down like this, these notions seem old-fashioned. Indeed they are, but unfortunately they are not obsolete.

Many managers still look for those old signs of ambition. "Fire in the belly," they call it. Some say, "She's a shark. She'll kill to get the business." Or, "He really wants it," never explaining what "it" is.

Most of the time, I think, all this intense talk of ambition gets to be a setup. Or it's a double setup. Either the shark is setting up the manager with a lot of expectations, or the manager is setting up the employee with a lot of expectations, or they're setting up one another.

Not that they're not sincere, it's just that they're sincere about something neither has defined: ambition.

In a society of ambition, how do you tell a young person to leave the ambition at the door, that it will only get in the way? You do it by redefining ambition, which must be done in terms of co-production or co-creation. The dark side of ambition is that it traditionally has been singular, self-aggrandizing, and demeaning of others. It often succeeds only if others fail. But in the community of work, if some fail, most fail, and all become victims.

There is a Lily Tomlin line: "We're all in this . . . alone."

A better line for business, though, is the one used by Larry Wilson at his Pecos River Conference Center: "I have to do it by myself, but I can't do it alone."

Success has never been different, not for business managers, not for generals, not for presidents, not for kings. No one has ever done it without other people's hard work and commitment; it's just that by the old definition of ambition, we were supposed to believe we did it on our own, the myth of the "self-made man."

The new definition of ambition still begins with self-interest, as it always has, then adds another dimension.

Indeed, make something of yourself, try your best to get to the top, if that's where you want to go, but know that *the more people you try to take along with you, the faster you'll get there and the longer you'll stay there.*

LEAVING IT ALL BEHIND

There were days when we still didn't get it,
that this wasn't like school or the military,
that we wouldn't graduate or get out
and leave it all behind.
We brought lunches in brown paper bags
and folded airplanes
to fly in the park,
and lusted after secretaries
just in from the small towns
and still learning how to dress.

We pitied the older guys
playing out their big-time businessman roles
as if most of them were not just some kind
of free-market bureaucrats.
Somehow we knew we'd do better
and we knew we'd be different,
without that need to cover our asses,
without that fear of failure.
We would give young guys like us
plenty of room to make us look good,
and we would ignore stupid policies and politics
and get rid of deadwood vice presidents
who wasted time and money and office space.
We would have the guts to take our money and run
before the job pushed us too hard
and the next title became too important,
before we found ourselves on airplanes every week
and in the office every weekend,
before our kids stopped caring if we were around,
and our wives drank too much
at too many ladies' luncheons
where they were going to have just a sherry
or one glass of wine,
before we got tired of smiling at every jerk
who might spend a dime with us,

before we ate every oversauced meal
and sniffed every cork and drank every bottle of
   wine,
before we went to every sunny resort
and heard every self-improvement speaker
and danced at every black-tie dinner
and applauded every chairman and program
   committee
and carried home every printed tote bag
and monogrammed vinyl notebook
and T-shirt,
and put every smiling group picture in a scrapbook.

Before all that,
we would get out.

James A. Autry

LIGHTS FLASHING AT O'HARE

Taxiing in on United at O'Hare
you see fire engines and an ambulance,
lights flashing,
and you think of snowy mornings
in a trailer somewhere in France,
near a runway of accelerating sounds,
loud but comforting in their consistency.
Then nothing,
and before you remember that silence
is not what you want to hear,
that fear born of something much older than
    airplanes
rises like a siren in your brain,
who who who who who?

In your briefcase is a calendar
filled for months to come,
time stretching like a chore
as far as you can turn the pages,
another week another year
to be played out in meetings and memos and trips.
Then, looking back toward the flashing lights,
ready by the runway,
you realize that out there somewhere
some poor son of a bitch
just wants the next five minutes
to be over.

THE ANGLER

He angled his way around New York,
always crossing diagonally,
never at the corners,
proud of saving a thousand miles of shoe leather
over his forty years of selling.

In the beginning, he called himself a drummer,
then a peddler with a shine,
and lately, a seller,
telling his drinking buddies, "We're all sellers,
no matter what you think you do."

He drummed and peddled and sold himself
into a nice club,
a house worth ten times what he paid
back when Greenwich was a sleepy town,
and a place on a golf course in Georgia.

He phones less now, writes fewer letters
than when he first made the move South
and called to check on us,
making sure we were keeping our noses clean
and the value of his stock high.
And he no longer invites us down for golf,
to sleep in the guest room and talk of old times,
realizing at last there are no angles into memory,
that we are remembered or forgotten
for things too late to change.

STILL CHOOGLIN' AFTER ALL THESE YEARS

It was not the palm trees
or surf,
another paradise meeting
in a long list,
that brought the sudden shift.
But something put us together again
for the first time in a long time.
The music perhaps,
or David saying,
"These children don't choogle like we did,"
burnished our friendship
like an old and precious thing
stored away and not often remembered,
a treasure taken for granted,
sometimes handled carelessly
like those heirlooms you move in boxes
from house to house
and never seem to find a place for.
Something about the paradise
and the band
and the baby boomers dancing
and David saying, in his country-boy voice,
"Let's go show them young 'uns how to shake their
        booties,"
and we found ourselves in it again,
immersed and rising in the affection
of twenty years of giving it all we've got,
deadlines, planes, meetings,
celebrating a new product,
consoling ourselves about a failure,
fighting and losing touch,
feeling apart, betrayed, angry.
Yet in that wet night,
laughing at our potbellies and ancient dance steps,
we knew that what we've gone through
meant more than we ever thought it could.

PART II

CHANGING THE WORDS: CHANGING THE WORK

We Are What We Say

I HAVE a friend, a poet and teacher, who says, "Change a metaphor, change the world."

Becoming a manager has much to do with learning the metaphors; becoming a good manager has much to do with using the metaphors; and becoming a leader has much to do with changing the metaphors.

But in business we tend to pay more attention to jargon than to metaphors. The metaphors are there—all around us, in fact—but it is difficult to grasp their power. To do so, however, is to be able to mold the workplace and the business to our own goals—just by the way we think and talk.

In our instinct for the obvious, we usually just accept the transitory conventional wisdoms, stuff like, "Everything is going upscale," or "Niche marketing is the future," or "We're seeing the return of traditional values," or whatever the business press is saying these days. We've seen, just in the past ten years, the business press go from "productivity" to "quality" to "customer service" as *the* formula for success.

It is not that these conventional wisdoms are untrue or

unimportant; to the contrary, they all are important in their own time, and they all contribute to success.

But this pop talk has little to do with the powerful metaphors of business and their influence on how a business manages its employees and presents itself in the community at large.

We learned in school that a metaphor is a figure of speech, the "application of a word or phrase to something that it does not apply to literally, as *the evening of one's life*."

That definition was okay for high school, but it ignores the transformative power of a metaphor, the power that can change the way we think about our world, our work, our lives.

For instance, when a company says, "Quality is our number-one product," the company is either lying or using a metaphor to change perceptions by its employees and its customers. Obviously, quality is not a product; it is an attribute of a product.

Just as obviously, there's no such thing as friendly skies.

Or the heartbeat of America.

Or the wings of man.

Or reaching out to touch someone over the telephone.

And do managers really mean it when they talk about kicking ass in the marketplace?

Or busting through the line?

Or working on our blocking and tackling?

Or hitting the bull's-eye?

Or building a new team?

Or hiring young sharks?

Or getting rid of deadwood?

And do the employees really mean it when they say it's a jungle out there?

Or he's a slave driver?

Or this place is the pits?

Or the salt mine?

Or the treadmill?

All these things are only metaphors. They aren't really true.

Or are they?

Could it be that they are true but just not literally accurate? Could it be that by saying these things, companies and managers and employees *make* them true?

By this time, you know that I believe the answer is "D. Yes to all the above."

We do make things true by what we say. Plato realized that a posture of pretense can also have some very real ramifications. A working commitment toward the "lie" of something can create the conditions that will make that something a reality.

Things *and* people are what we call them, because in the simplest terms, we are what we say, and others are what we say about them. Words, after all, are powerful symbols of ideas. For those of us who do not paint or sculpt or compose music or dance or excel at athletics, words are the most powerful symbols we have.

In the workplace, words are our most frequent tool, and the leader's words can work magic, can change the environment and the work and the morale, and can create a whole new way of thinking.

For instance, I believe we businesspeople must stop thinking dualistically of our lives and our jobs. We must stop thinking of work as something imposed upon us by the need to make money, and think of it as something we have chosen to participate in because of its value in our lives and in the community at large. In other words, we must stop "going to work" or "staying home" but must think of our lives as a continuum of endeavor, a collection of *works* making up a larger work that is our lives.

This is, of course, changing our own personal metaphors, which is a first and necessary step to changing metaphors for others. Then, as leaders, we can begin using metaphors that, in my view, are in the greatest long-term interest of business.

In another essay in this book, I have joked about sports metaphors, but stay with me while I offer a more serious look.

A team, by popular definition, is a group organized to work together to accomplish certain objectives, most of which are relatively short term. Of course, the full definition of "team" goes well beyond that, but think less of the technical definition and more of its metaphorical use in the workplace.

Certainly, there have been, and to some extent still are, positive aspects of being on a team, having team spirit, and cooperating with the other team members. But team athletics, in its increasing professionalism extending now into the schools, and in its accelerating emphasis on superstars and cult figures, is rapidly losing its place in our mythology as the font of true-blue heroes and "sportsmanship."

By invoking the metaphor of sports teams these days, we imply that we in business are involved in a game in which there must be winners and losers, in which there are stars who play and benchwarmers who watch, in which our personal success is measured only by the numbers on the scoreboard and not by how well we played, and in which our value to society is transitory at best.

A community, by popular definition, is a group of people living in one geographical area. The dictionary also says community is a group of people bound by common interests or origins. And the word "fellowship" is used.

By invoking the metaphor of community, we imply that we in business are bound by a fellowship of endeavor in which we commit to mutual goals, in which we contribute to the best of our abilities, in which each contribution is recognized and credited, in which there is a forum for all voices to be heard, in which our success contributes to the success of the common enterprise and to the success of others, in which we can disagree and hold differing viewpoints without withdrawing from the community, in which we are free to express what we feel as well as what we think, in which our value to society is directly related to the quality of our commitment and effort, and in which we take care of one another.

All this is high-sounding, to be sure, but we intend metaphors as *inspiration to make things as they are not now but should be.* In the context of community, all life is possible and necessary, the pleasant and unpleasant, the conflict and the cooperation, the celebration of those who succeed personally and the pain of those who don't.

I do not contend that the metaphor of community will work for all businesses at this time. Perhaps team works well for your enterprise; perhaps the short-term action you need now is best produced by a team.

The time will come, sooner or later, when your team players will realize that winning always comes at the end of the game, but there is no end to the work. At that point, work looks a lot more like life—a process that requires us to make the most of it every day and to concentrate on the journey, not the destination.

When your team reaches that point, you'll need another metaphor. Be prepared.

How About Some New Titles?

As my beliefs about management and the new workplace evolve, I increasingly come head-to-head with the residue of the old governmental/military paradigm of organizational structure. In the language, in the policy manuals, in the titles, in the department names.

Some defenders of the present organization would point out that business *has* changed. After all, they'd say, most companies no longer call the personnel department the personnel department. They call it the human resources department. The problem is, human resources department sounds even worse. I want to be a person and I want to be thought of as a person, not as a human resource, for God's sake. I'd even rather be a personnel, whatever that is. Human resources, as a term, is an extension of the old system—and simply reinforces the fact that it is the skills of the human that traditionally have interested the company, not the *humanness* of the human.

Recently, however, if we can believe the popular business books, the humanness, even the humanity, of the human has become a resource, particularly in management. I support this new attitude, to every extent it may be true, and beyond.

If it is true, and not just lip service, I suggest that there is a good way to communicate a company's commitment to the new paradigm: redesign the titles, of the departments and of the people.

Start with the human resources department. Most HR departments are divided into placement, training, compensation and benefits, and employee relations.

In the new workplace, the overall department becomes the *human development department*. Has a ring to it, and it's filled with all kinds of meaning.

Placement becomes the *talent department*. The placement people could be called the talent scouts.

Training becomes *growth*; compensation and benefits becomes *recognition and reward*. We need a department to attend to the things we never anticipate but always come up, so I'd have the employee relations department incorporate that by making it the *department of employee needs and concerns*.

All companies have a chief executive officer, and many have a chief operating officer. Okay. But how about calling the present human resources VP the chief caring officer? Just imagine the business card: John S. Smith, vice president/chief caring officer. Or simply vice president/caring. Not bad.

Surely, there's a place in today's company for a renewal manager and a growth manager and a special treatment specialist. In the auditing department, we could have a fun auditor, to make sure everyone is having enough.

You get the idea. But I know I'm not being very realistic. I know that titles are important to many people in business, particularly those who have them, and I know that titles don't change very easily. In fact, I know that changing the titles is a lot less important that changing the way we think about our relationships, both departmental and individual.

So I'll settle for that. Relationships first, titles later. Okay?

New Age or Common Sense?

AFTER I spoke at a business-school seminar on management recently, one of the participants said to me, "You sound like one of those New Age managers I've read about."

I didn't need to ask what he meant or what he had read; his tone of voice said it all: weekends of group therapy, meditation and "stress management" workshops, guided imagery, expressive dance to Far Eastern harmonies played on lutes and wooden flutes, self-esteem workshops, lessons in the soft martial arts, and reflections on the spiritual aspects of work.

As flakey as all this may sound, I have participated in most of it. If nothing else, it is difficult to think of myself as a corporate biggie while I'm trying expressive dance. It helps keep the humility intact.

On the other hand, I think these pursuits are just another way to cast off some of the anachronistic conventional wisdoms of business in order to arrive at new ways of thinking about management. The new ways, I believe, involve common sense more than anything else. If that is New Age, so be it.

Rather than leave the impression that the spiritual journey

of management has to be thought of in a mystical way, however, I set forth here seven principles and seven corollaries that I believe form the basis of common-sense management.

Principle

1. Every person is intrinsically worthwhile.

2. All workers deserve the opportunity to succeed to their highest potential.

3. All workers deserve to be listened to and heard.

4. People will do a good job because they want to do a good job.

5. Compassion for, and sensitivity to, the individual is the basis for creating the most productive working environment.

6. The community succeeds because of its members' commitment to shared goals and values.

7. Hard work and honesty beat guile and politics every time.

Corollary

1. Not everybody's function in the workplace has equal worth to the common enterprise. Every job is important, but not every *job* has equal value. This, however, has nothing to do with the worth of people.

2. Not all workers want the opportunity to succeed to their highest potential.

3. A manager is not obligated to act on everything a worker says or suggests.

4. Not everyone wants to do a good job.

5. Sensitivity and responsiveness to the individual should not outweigh the long-term welfare of the group.

6. Not every member is committed to the same extent to those goals and values.

7. Hard work and honesty succeed only if they are not so self-righteous that they reject thoughtful compromise.

There are no rules in these principles, only ways of thinking about people and the workplace. There are no answers, no surefire means for determining who has the commitment or who wants to do a good job or who wants only to put in his time without regard for achieving anyone's notion of "highest potential."

And there certainly are no formulas for making that most difficult of decisions about balancing the good of the individual and the good of the group. The hard choices and judgments remain where they always have: right on the manager's shoulders.

Common sense is the best guide, but it doesn't hurt to realize that the whole thing sometimes is a dance as well as a balancing act, and that a little meditation and stress management, a little closing of the eyes and visualizing what to do next, or a little reflection on the spiritual nature of your role as manager might just go a long way toward making the right judgment.

Irreverent Thoughts About Organization Charts

In almost thirty-five years of organizational life, I've never figured out what useful purpose organization charts serve, and if I had my choice, we'd do away with them.

But they seem so firmly embedded into the consciousness of every American, from Boy Scouts to school boards to corporations, that I know organization charts will outlive me. All I can do is warn everyone who'll listen: Learn and remember the laws of organization charts:

1. They mainly are about egos, and they serve to inflate egos in a roughly ten-to-one inverse ratio with the egos they deflate.

2. An organization chart, posted in an obvious place, is a proven morale killer.

3. Organization charts are *always* inaccurate, even as some poor bored secretary is carefully lining out the new one and sending it off for photocopying. And if the chart is not inaccurate, the organization does not have enough change, thus is in big trouble.

4. Organization charts in a company neither define relationships as they actually exist nor direct the lines of com-

munication. People do all this for themselves, and the realities of relationships and lines of communication never match the charts. When you find the rare company in which the charts do define relationships and do direct lines of communication, sell your stock at once. There's not an ounce of imagination in the whole place.

If the "organization" does not exist in the minds and hearts of the people, it does not exist. No chart can fix that. An organization's function is simple: to provide a framework, a format, a context in which people can effectively use resources to accomplish their goals.

Among their most important resources are their relationships with one another. Who's on top and who's on bottom, according to the chart, is among the least important information. Besides, we all know who the boss is, and our employees know who we are.

So why make a diagram out of the obvious?

The Way We Talk

SHOW ME someone who says "utilize" instead of "use," and I'll show you someone who says "individual" instead of "person."

Much has been written about jargon and how it characterizes different areas of endeavor. Critics say jargon is used as a discriminatory tool, to shut out those with whom the "in" group does not wish to communicate. Other criticism has focused on jargon as pretense and self-aggrandizement.

I agree with these criticisms, but I suggest also that they miss two dangers that represent important problems for management: The first is that the momentum of this ever-emerging business vocabulary is more and more toward technocratic, rather than personal, ways of speaking and writing. Simply stated, it leaves out people and personal references.

With all the railing against Washington bureaucracy and bureau-babble, we in business fall into the same traps. We're always "interfacing" and "dialoguing." I've even heard businesspeople "surfacing some issues," and most everyone "accesses" information from time to time.

The second danger is that we are patterning the language

to be flat and unexpressive. Just as sloppy language demonstrates sloppy thinking, so flat and unexpressive language demonstrates flat and unexpressive thinking.

In marketing, we went from talking about our products with their "unique selling proposition" to "positioning" our products in the marketplace. Now, with the "commodification" of our products and the accompanying cost/price pressures, we talk about being "low-cost producers."

There seems to be some mystique attached to using more syllables when fewer would do.

There is no doubt that business needs a fresh vocabulary that recognizes the emotional aspects of business and work and that is closer to the way people feel and talk about their feelings.

Ideas flow in an open and unstilted environment in which things are identified as what they are, and in which people express themselves without resorting to code.

But it is obvious that we in business often have invented our language to mislead, to hide behind, or simply to reinforce the conventional wisdoms.

Let me close with an old favorite, one with which all good business people of the right attitude are supposed to agree. The next time you hear that old saw, "There are no problems, only opportunities," tell 'em this:

"Baloney! No one can find a solution to an opportunity. There are problems, and unless we call them problems, we'll never solve them."

Learning the Truth
About Power

I USED to think the company could give me power. My boss could just say, "Autry, we're promoting you to head of the editorial group, which means, of course, you now have what you've always wanted—power."

I'm not sure why I had wanted power or what it really meant to me, except this: It meant power *over* others, power to get people to do what *I* said was right, rather than what *they* thought was right.

It took me a long time to realize that the company could give me only authority, not power. And those two are not even close to being the same thing. The purpose of authority has more to do with influence and less to do with power.

There is power, of course. A lot of power in our society accrues to those with money or with access to money. Power accrues to some elected officials. And power *does indeed* accrue to managers, but it does not come from where most managers think it comes from.

The management challenge is *not* in getting people to *be* the way you want them to be, it is in getting them to *do* what you know they must do to accomplish the shared goals of the group.

As Tom Gould, CEO of Younkers, a chain of department stores in the Midwest, says, "While you can control a small, finite number of people, you can influence an infinite number."

A manager must understand this about power and control: Power comes only from the people you manage. They give it to you because they trust you to use it well, and if you don't use it well, they take it away from you. And you'll hardly know it happened.

I had to test my power several times before I realized where it came from. The test went like this:

In a meeting one day, I said, "Okay, folks, I want you to go out and do this thing just the way I say."

"But, Jim," they answered, "it won't work."

"Take my word for it," I said. "It'll work."

They continued to resist, so finally I said, "Just do it as I said. You'll see."

Guess what? In a few days, they came back and, standing almost limp-wristed, said something like, "Gee, Jim, we tried it just the way you said. . . . Didn't work."

I was telling this story over dinner to a friend who is CEO of a major financial institution. In response, he told me how he finally had learned the power-versus-influence lesson. The subject was operating hours. My friend felt his company's hours of operation should expand to be of more service to the customer. But the idea of expanded hours threatened to be so disruptive that he ran into great resistance from the company officers.

"They came up with every conceivable reason not to do it, from cost to morale," he said, "so I had to try patience. I started asking, 'How can we serve our customers better?,' and the staff would come up with good ideas. We'd implement those ideas, then I'd ask again, 'How can we serve our customers better?,' and they'd come up with more ideas. Finally, I asked, 'If we are to serve our customers the best we can, what hours must we be open?' And the employees began to set the hours.

"It may take us a year longer to get there," my friend concluded, "but when we are staying open seven days a week, it will be *their* decision."

My friend's wisdom demonstrated a valuable lesson in power and control versus influence.

Power and control are illusions that we create for ourselves out of the sense of our authority, just as we have the illusion that we control our children because we're bigger and stronger. At some point, we realize the truth: Our children control their own lives, and all we can hope to do is influence them.

The same is true with your employees. The power you have is the willingness and commitment of your employees to carry out your goals or vision. And they have that commitment because they trust you to lead them in the right way. You do not have the power to force them to do well the things they don't agree with.

Furthermore, the power you have—which they have given you—is to be used *for* them. As the head of a group of committed people who share and support your vision, you have enormous power: in the marketplace and within your company.

But do not try to use the power *against* your people, as so many managers do. You'll just waste a lot of time and effort establishing what you'll realize finally is an illusion. You'll also realize finally that your employees weren't suffering under that same illusion.

The Truth About Data

HERE ARE two big lies of the technological age: Lie number one: Computers and computerized information systems save on paperwork. Truth: They create paperwork. Lie number two: Computer-generated data makes decision-making easier. Truth: Data has very little to do with decision-making. (I refuse to use "data" as a plural noun.)

I once heard a very smart businessman say that, sooner or later, all business decisions get down to what your instincts tell you to do.

Another way to think of instincts is as wisdom, the accumulation of what we have learned, consciously and subconsciously, all of our lives—and if you believe the mystics, even before.

In the quest for "better information," we as managers have become almost enslaved by data processing and the ensuing endless analyses.

Computers have their place. My business would have great difficulty without them, but I refuse to sign on to the widespread statement "Our business couldn't survive without them."

One of the managers I respect most has a question he asks when someone says something is impossible.

"Impossible, or merely inconvenient?" he asks.

Our business would be terribly inconvenienced without computers, but we couldn't *survive* without people who can make decisions based on their instincts. Computers can't make decisions based on anything. The weakest excuse in business today is, "According to the data, it should have worked."

I have a little litany I say whenever someone tries to blame it on the computer:

Data is not facts.
Facts are not information.
Information is not knowledge.
Knowledge is not truth.
Truth is not wisdom.

Any decision you can make based on what is revealed by data and information is a decision that can be delegated.

Any decision requiring data and information, plus knowledge, is a decision you can train other knowledgeable people to make.

But it is in the realm of truth and wisdom that most critical decisions are made. And those are the ones that can only come from you, after you have weighed all the data and information, applied your knowledge, and then reached down deep into your gut, your instincts, your wisdom.

Understand that your ability to do this is your true value as an executive/manager/leader, a value not likely to be superseded by technology.

Everybody Talkin' 'Bout Heaven Ain't Goin' There

THE TITLE is a line from a spiritual they used to sing down South where I grew up, and it applies to so many situations in business that I hardly know where to use it first.

But I've chosen "ethics."

Everybody talkin' 'bout ethics these days. Business schools now teach graduate-level courses in ethics. Companies have broken out in codes of ethics, most of which make sure no one will do what very few would ever be tempted to do anyway, and most of which are loose enough to permit what the situation requires.

So here's the truth about business ethics: There is no such thing as business ethics, only people ethics.

Business, as a force and as an impersonal entity behind which we can hide, will compromise any ethical standard, if left to its own natural momentum, because there is nothing inherently ethical in a free market, in free enterprise, or in the capitalistic system. Nor in any other system, for that matter.

A company code of ethics is valuable only to the extent it reflects the attitudes of top management about the kind of moral judgment required of employees. The most helpful code of ethics I can imagine is this:

We will be fair, sensitive, honest, trusting, and trustworthy in all our dealings among ourselves, with customers, with vendors, and with the community at large. We will obey all laws, in fact and in spirit, and we will always do the right thing, in every situation, to the best of our abilities. And if we fail, we will do whatever is required to make amends.

Ethics is a subset of morality that exists only among people, not among institutions, not among systems, not among organizations. So the "code" must be within every employee. If the people don't behave ethically, neither can the company.

Talkin' 'bout heaven just isn't good enough.

The Problem with Policies

A COUPLE of years ago, I asked one of my group vice presidents to help me comb through all our policies and get rid of the silly ones.

"How will I know the silly ones?" he asked.

"Easy," I said. "They're the ones written to keep everybody from doing what only a few people would do—and they'll do it anyway."

Did you ever notice that about policies? While there are good ones with helpful procedures or with information about laws and regulations, most policies are restrictive devices aimed at keeping people *from* doing things, rather than enabling or empowering devices that help people *to* do things.

The problem is that policies have served for years as the easy way out for cowardly management. Rather than confronting people who do not embrace the common vision and work toward it—in other words, the people who don't do the job as it should be done—management writes a policy.

It reminds me of a story a school-superintendent friend once told me. He said that one of the high school teachers in his rural district was wearing exceedingly revealing clothes. Her inappropriate dress was causing classroom problems with the teenaged male students.

"She either was oblivious to the problem," my friend said, "or she didn't give a damn. So I told the principal to speak with her about the teachers' dress code.

"About two more weeks passed, then the principal called me, asking what to do. The situation was no better. 'Did you speak with her?' I asked. 'Yes," he said, but later I found out he had called a faculty meeting and addressed the subject to the entire group. He didn't confront her personally."

It was so much like business, I had to laugh. How typical to berate the group for what one or two workers may be doing, particularly when the manager knows exactly who is causing the problem. The result is that the manager manages to anger the innocent employees while letting the guilty ones believe that if everyone is catching the heat, they're safe.

If the guilty persist, then the manager probably will write a policy. It is this gutlessness that produces so many silly policies.

I believe this: There *are* problem people in the world. Some of them have worked for me, and some of them have probably worked for you. When the problem person inevitably shows up in your employ, you have but one choice: Go straight to the source and try to help the person solve the problem. This includes doing honest, straightforward, and perhaps painful appraisals, setting performance standards, and giving old-fashioned constructive criticism regularly—along with frequent offers of your personal help.

Constructive criticism is not mystical. It can be as simple as saying, "Your sales presentations will improve considerably if you cut out all but the essential sales points," then handing the person a presentation you've edited or otherwise improved. Demonstrating how something can be done better is the best constructive criticism. Then say, "But you don't have to accept my version; why don't you take mine and make it even more effective?" This avoids the I'm-smarter-than-you-because-I'm-the-boss syndrome.

Constructive criticism also includes setting deadlines for improvement and, perhaps, putting the person on probation. If all this effort proves unsuccessful, fire the person.

But do not perpetrate another silly policy.

Keeping Secrets

THE WHOLE subject of confidential information would be very troublesome in a company if it weren't at the same time so humorous and, for that matter, so moot.

There are no secrets. There may be proprietary information, which is guarded by all kinds of controls; there may be insider strategic and financial information, which doesn't make its way around the halls; but in my observation, the reason those things are known by only a limited number of people is that no one else is all that interested.

In all the management positions I've held over the years, I've generally learned more from the grapevine than from those "Personal and Confidential/To be opened by addressee only" memos.

So why all the secrecy? Simple: It's power. Somewhere someone got the notion, and passed it along, that power accrues to those with the secrets.

Of course, it follows that power is no good unless someone knows you have it. How does that someone find out you have it? Simple: You tell the secrets.

You say, "What I'm about to tell you is very confidential;

of course I know you'll keep it that way." At that point, whatever it is no longer qualifies as a secret. The next person cannot demonstrate power without doing what you've just done: tell the secret.

It doesn't matter, of course, because by then a lot of other people already know.

A preoccupation with the secrets gets in the way of good management from time to time. Some managers use the sharing of confidential information to show a certain employee that he or she is held in particular esteem. Then, of course, the only way the employee can let the other employees know about this favored status with the boss is to tell the secret. We all know how well that goes down with the other employees.

The problems frequently occur in the backlash that happens when employees begin to learn the secrets, as they inevitably do and in their own ways.

"Why didn't management trust us enough to let us in on it, without our hearing it from the grapevine?" A good question, one I've been asked in all-employee meetings; I've never had a good answer, because usually there was no good reason.

It is the same in the military. There are many classifications for information, but the most irritating and demoralizing one is referred to as "Need to Know." In other words, someone of a higher rank is always deciding what those of a lower rank "need to know," and if there are those who are not on a "need to know basis," they don't get to know. Imagine how they feel. They are presumably fit and ready to risk their lives for their country, but somebody in headquarters decides what they do or don't need to know about that eventuality.

Sometimes business is not much different. We are asking people to commit, to embrace the vision, to develop a sense of ownership—all those currently hip concepts of management—but we don't trust these people enough to open up and tell them what's going on.

This is not to say that there are never reasons to keep some kinds of information confidential; to the contrary, there are two kinds of reasons for keeping information confidential: legal and ethical. The legal stuff is clear-cut, at least to the extent that the legal department will help you with the decision. The ethical concerns are more complicated, but I believe the only real ethical information issues involve the invasion of individual employees' privacy. I commend to you good sense as the best guide.

As for the rest of it, be guided by this rule: *An employee cannot have too much information.* Every employee has the need to know—as much as possible. The more everyone understands what you and the department and the company are up to, the more commitment you'll get.

Looking for the Easy Way Out

THERE IS a Japanese riddle: "Who must do the difficult things?" Answer: "Those who can."

Doing the hard things is almost the one-phrase definition of management. The "hard things," of course, always involve dealing with people. Everything else—capital, equipment, resources of one sort or another—is easy compared to the people problems.

So, naturally, a lot of managers look for ways to avoid doing the hard things. In my observation, the prospect of facing a problem person head-on is often the mother of creativity.

One easy way out of a people problem is to *reorganize*. A shift here or there, a new organization chart, announcement memos, an article in the company newsletter, and the hard thing is put off on someone else, usually a lower-level manager or another department head.

Another technique is to create a new job. We've seen it a hundred times—suddenly, the department needs a "coordinator" of something or other. Then the next time the manager faces a problem person, the department is already set up to need an "associate coordinator" of something or other. Then an "assistant coordinator," and so on until there is a subgroup coordination department. When this happens, of course, the original "coordinator" gets to thinking the job is vital and asks for a raise, thus creating another problem. I will leave for your imagination how then he becomes "vice president/coordination."

This kind of maneuvering usually occurs when a manager is trying to deal with someone who works hard, who wants to succeed, and who gives it every effort, but who *just doesn't get it*. It may be that the person is not very smart; perhaps it's a matter of awareness or sensitivity; more likely it is that the person is working at his or her capacity and simply is limited.

We have to face and accept this reality. Some people, after all the training and support you can give, will only achieve an "acceptable" performance.

In the process of evaluating people, we tend toward the extremes of outstanding performance and abject failure, when we know that most of us fall somewhere in the middle. We know also that the greater the success of the group, the higher the standards become.

Thus the hard dilemma when someone just can't meet a new expectation.

It happened to one of my group's young managers not long ago. I got an urgent telephone message. He had to see me. His first words in the door were, "I've got to fire Joel."

"Isn't it kind of sudden?" I asked. "Nine months ago, you said he was brilliant."

"That was before I learned as much about his area as I know now. And he just doesn't make the right calculations."

"What else does he not do?" I asked.

"Isn't that enough?" he asked.

"You mean he makes mistakes that reflect in the results of his department?" I asked.

"Not that so much. I just don't think he asks enough questions, so I don't think he gets the right assumptions for his calculations."

By this time, I understood that the manager was judging Joel by his own superior abilities to see many subtleties in a given situation and to ask extraordinarily insightful questions that frequently then led to better, more enlightened assumptions.

"In other words," I said, "he's not as good as you."

"Well, I guess that's partly it."

"But if he were, I would have given him your job and left you where you were. I don't expect him to have your unusual turn of mind, and you shouldn't either."

"But it's frustrating to be explaining all this to him all the time. He just doesn't seem to get it."

"And you think you can find someone out there who will get it without the training you'll have to give? Absurd."

"You may be right, but I don't think Joel will ever get it."

"All you can do is judge his results overall and figure out what he does well, so you won't drive yourself crazy worrying about what he can't do. Of course, if he is not producing the results overall, then we'll discuss other measures."

"Do I just ignore the problem? I can't do that."

"Of course not. You have to tell him what you feel the shortcomings are. Tell him he doesn't get it, that his questions lack imagination and that this causes him to do very pedestrian calculations."

"But that's like telling him I think he's not very smart." He was clearly distressed.

"Is it better," I asked, "to keep from him your opinion of his questions, assumptions, and calculations? How can you do that and give him an honest appraisal? You don't owe him an outstanding rating, but you do owe him honesty. You also owe him help and training until you're positive it's futile. Even if he never becomes as smart as you think he should be, he does not deserve to be fired."

Then the manager said it: "I think it would be easier to fire him than to tell him that I don't think he's smart enough."

And I said, "Welcome to management."

Unless I miss my guess, I'll be seeing a proposed-reorganization memo any day now.

Block That Metaphor

OKAY, I admit it. I was drum major of my college band.

But I don't think that's the reason I've had it up to here with all the damned sports metaphors big-time business managers like to use.

I admit I'm not confused when they say, at some business meeting, "We've got to concentrate on the basics, on our blocking and our tackling." It would be silly for me to point out that nobody in our company does anything remotely resembling blocking or tackling. But perhaps no sillier than suggesting that those sports metaphors are instructive in helping us be better at whatever we do.

I can't imagine what the women think when some CEO switches on the old halftime speech: "Just take the ball, put your head down, and run right through them."

We know what it means, of course. It means that most managers believe that business in itself does not contain the drama, the action, or the excitement of a football game, so they try to jazz up the action with all the old sports clichés even as those pep talks become less and less relevant to the new workers, particularly women.

I say the very least we should be able to expect these days is some variety in our metaphors, so in the interest of providing a useful all-occasion vocabulary for the manager who, like me, is uncomfortable trying to sound like the business-school version of Vince Lombardi, let me call on my old band background to suggest the following:

Instead of telling them to watch their blocking and tackling, say, "Concentrate at all times on your intonation." They might have trouble applying that to a sales call, but no more so than blocking and tackling.

Or tell them, "Think about your embouchure and breathe from the diaphram." That's really pretty good advice for any speaking situation. Besides, you'll send a lot of them scurrying for their dictionaries, and that's not all bad in itself.

What about calling it "ensemble" instead of "teamwork?" Or saying something like, "Let's make this a *molto fortissimo* presentation."

Of course, we *could* forget about metaphors altogether and just talk about our business as if it really is as exciting or uplifting or fun as a ball game. Or a musical performance.

Winning Redefined

As I write this, I am winging my way from one sales meeting to another and thinking about how one of our managers just handled a group meeting.

"I'm into winning," she said, seeking to inspire the team toward another successful year, "so let's get out there and kick butt."

Why is it, I wonder, that being into winning means also being into someone else losing? Dr. Betty Sue Flowers, of the University of Texas, suggests, "In this culture, we always need an enemy to define who we are."

There is no doubt that people respond to the win/lose model to the point that seeing the competition "lose" is sometimes as important as winning.

I've heard salespeople say, "Well, we didn't get the business, but neither did they."

And people seem universally more enthusiastic about "winning" when they know the other group "lost."

The only problem is that, by the traditional definition, no one wins all the time in business. No one. Your turn to "lose" comes regardless of how good you are.

I like to quote one of my favorite management books, which, among other helpful things, says this: "The race is neither to the swift nor the battle to the strong . . . but time and chance happeneth to them all."

Put another way, the other guys may win next year no matter how good you are or how bad you think they are.

And consider this: You've probably been in the losing position before but never believed it, and neither does anyone else. No manager ever said, "We're a bunch of losers." No good manager anyway. *A good manager redefines the terms, then sets new goals.* Even ball teams refer to their continued losses as "being in a slump."

So it is an illusion to take joy or satisfaction in identifying the losers, because unless they believe it, *they're not losers.* And therein lies an important perception for all of us.

I would not for a minute want to undermine whatever it is that keeps employees in high spirits and focused on succeeding, but let me try another definition of "winning." Take it or leave it.

Winning is doing something that exceeds beyond what you'd hoped it would.

Winning is doing excellent work.

Winning is accomplishing goals for yourself and for the company, defined in your own terms, not in comparative terms, such as "I will achieve a five share-point gain," *not* "I will be five points better than . . ."

Winning is a matter of growth, personally and with your colleagues.

Winning is more how you feel about what you do and less about what you do.

PART III

MANAGING AND FEELING

It's Not Just Okay to Cry, It's Absolutely Necessary

SEVERAL YEARS ago, I was on a panel with a well-known management consultant in the publishing business. It was at the time when a lot of women were first coming into advertising and advertising sales.

A middle-aged man asked the consultant, "What do you do when you are appraising or criticizing a women and she starts crying?"

It was one of those questions frequently asked at that time by middle-aged men who, I surmised, either were having a lot of trouble with crying female employees or (more likely) thought they were going to have trouble with female employees they had not yet even hired.

Implicit in the question, of course, were a couple of things: One, the man implied that crying was somehow outside the rulebook, not allowed, not legitimate, thus its possibility justified whatever residual resentment he felt for women being in his business to begin with. And two, he implied that a crying employee created a management situation requiring some kind of special training.

The consultant had an answer: "I keep a box of Kleenex in

my office," he said, "and when a woman begins to cry, I just take out the box, put it in front of her, and leave the office until she regains control."

Please understand that I did not make up this quote to fit this essay. The man actually said it.

So I asked, "What do you do when a man cries?" Everyone laughed, thinking it was a quip. And my question never was answered.

The big-time consultant was wrong with his run-and-hide technique. He was wrong then, and he sure as hell would be wrong today.

Consider this: *If you don't think people, including you, should be able to cry about the job, then you don't think work is as important as you say it is.*

The subject, of course, is not crying but expressing emotion.

Many managers seem born with three emotional settings: pissed off, pouting, and pacified. You'd think that with such a narrow emotional range, these managers' moods would be easy to predict. Unfortunately, the opposite is true; the very narrowness of the range means that the manager's acceptable repertoire of emotions is so inadequate that one doesn't "fit" or "work" in enough situations—so most of the time the employees don't know which setting to expect from one day to the next.

I have a simple rule with one exception: The emotion you feel is the most appropriate emotion to express. The exception is anger. I think anger is a luxury the good manager cannot afford to express. Displeasure, yes. Anger, no. Irritation, yes. Anger, no. Disappointment, yes. Anger, no.

If I believe in the appropriateness of emotion in the workplace and I believe in honesty, why exclude anger? Simple: Anger is too risky in that is is too easily used as a weapon and it is too vulnerable to misinterpretation.

Anger as a weapon frequently leads to humiliation, and humiliation is the one thing no employee will ever forgive you. Think about it: Of the longtime grudges or ill feelings you may still personally harbor, aren't they really about humiliation?

The late mythologist Joseph Campbell told Bill Moyers the

story of the Japanese samurai who set out to avenge the death
of his master. When he found the assassin and pulled his sword
and prepared to strike the avenging blow, the assassin spat in
the samurai's face. At that, the samurai sheathed his sword,
turned, and went home without killing the man. The reason:
The samurai had been made angry by the man's spitting, and
to kill the man in anger would have been for the wrong reason,
thus not honorable.

That story's truth for managers is that *you cannot act properly
when you act in anger*. So mine is a business decision: You
cannot afford to do something with such long-term negative
impact. It will come back to haunt you more than you'll ever
believe.

Yet, for all the macho myth about it, crying at the appropriate time never hurts you or your image. I recall, for instance, a fancy lunch for all our New York employees during
the holiday season several years ago. At the time, one of our
magazines was sponsoring free transportation and a free conference for farmers from all over the country to come to Des
Moines to learn more about diversification of crops. We had
received hundreds of letters of gratitude from farmers and their
families. Some of these letters were passed along to our CEO,
who at the time was Bob Burnett.

Bob was telling our New York people about some of the
letters. A small-town Missouri boy himself, Bob became quite
emotional as he quoted one that said, "We're starving out here,
and you people seem to be the only ones who care." He stopped
talking for several seconds, and the tears appeared.

And at that point, our New York employees gained another
sense of Bob Burnett, the man, and his values. His "image,"
not that he cared about it, was enhanced by revealing his
humanity.

If you saw the Public TV presentation of *In Search of Excellence*, you may recall an interview with a supervisor who had
just given a little award to one of his employees. Back in his office, he said, "You know," then he paused to wipe a tear before
continuing, "I love those people out there." To me, that said a
lot about excellence and how he is able to achieve it.

A few weeks ago, one of the senior managers in my group told me about a very difficult critique session he'd had with one of his women employees. He had hired her, with great expectations of an outstanding performance. Instead, she had not adjusted well to her new job, and her performance was lackluster. An appraisal and perhaps a "caring confrontation" were in order.

When he told her she was not doing the job well enough, she began to cry. She knew, she said, she was letting him down, and her own disappointment in herself embarrassed her. Thus she cried.

"What did you do?" I asked.

"What could I do? I felt terrible. I cried too," he said, and I couldn't help thinking about the big-time management consultant and his box of Kleenex.

In my view, that manager demonstrated two things: He cared enough about the work that he was willing to confront someone he had a special interest in, and he cared enough about her to be hurt that she was upset.

But let me make something clear: *I'm not talking about management for and by the wimps.* In fact, I am talking about the most difficult management there is, a management without emotional hiding places.

You just can no longer be the tough guy, and you also can't come on as the impassive, icewater-in-the veins "cool head." On the other hand, the kindly parent who listens-and-understands-but-does-nothing approach also won't work.

No, in every situation, you must lead with your real self, because if you're going to be on the leading edge of management, you sometimes must be on the emotional edge as well.

WHAT PERSONNEL HANDBOOKS NEVER TELL YOU

They leave a lot out of the personnel handbooks.
Dying, for instance.
You can find funeral leave
but you can't find dying.
You can't find what to do
when a guy you've worked with since you both
   were pups
looks you in the eye
and says something about hope and chemotherapy.
No phrases,
no triplicate forms,
no rating systems.
Seminars won't do it
and it's too late for a new policy on sabbaticals.

They don't tell you about eye contact
and how easily it slips away
when a woman who lost a breast
says, "They didn't get it all."
You can find essays on motivation
but the business schools
don't teach what the good manager says
to keep people taking up the slack
while someone steals a little more time
at the hospital.
There's no help from those tapes
you pop into the player
while you drive or jog.
They'd never get the voice right.

And this poem won't help either.
You just have to figure it out for yourself,
and don't ever expect to do it well.

The Caring Confrontation

WHEN I flew jet fighters in the air force, I would come in from a particularly tough flight, something like formation flying in bad weather at night, and think, Nothing in civilian life can ever require this kind of nerve.

I was wrong.

I can think of nothing as demanding of nerve, as gut-wrenching, or as emotionally debilitating as firing someone.

I lie awake the night before, I wish with all my heart that the person would walk in and resign, and I curse being in the position of having to commit this mayhem.

No amount of thoughtful, professional rationale helps. The knowledge of being in the right is no source of courage. Firing is a rotten job. It is so rotten, in fact, that many managers feel they can do it only with coolness or in anger.

This is where the old hard-nosed management style has the advantage. The manager who relies on this approach every day, who regularly uses anger or intimidation as one of his communications "tools," probably can sweep a lot of emotional litter under the rug of toughness.

On the other hand, maybe we need a new definition of

toughness, and maybe that definition has something to do with *caring enough to be tough.*

Because there's just one way to fire someone: with love and support and deep, deep regret. You must try as much as possible to make the act itself a caring confrontation.

Recognize that in any firing, there is some failure of management, but that failure, whatever it is, should not be exacerbated by your failure to care enough for the person involved. If you must err, let it be on the side of generosity.

James A. Autry

ON FIRING A SALESMAN

It's like a little murder,
taking his life,
his reason for getting on the train,
his lunches at Christ Cella,
and his meetings in warm and sunny places
where they all gather,
these smiling men,
in sherbet slacks and blue blazers,
and talk about business
but never about prices,
never breaking that law
about the prices they charge.

But what about the prices they pay?
What about gray evenings in the bar car
and smoke-filled clothes and hair
and children already asleep
and wives who say
"You stink"
when they come to bed?
What about the promotions they don't get,
the good accounts they lose
to some kid MBA
because somebody thinks their energy is gone?

What about those times they see in a mirror
or the corner of their eye
some guy at the club shake his head
when they walk through the locker room
the way they shook their heads years ago
at an old duffer
whose handicap had grown along with his age?

And what about this morning,
the summons,
the closed door,
and somebody shaved and barbered and shined

fifteen years their junior
trying to put on a sad face
and saying he understands?

A murder with no funeral,
nothing but those quick steps outside the door,
those set jaws,
those confident smiles,
that young disregard for even the thought
of a salesman's mortality.

James A. Autry

CORNERED

Armed with a cup of coffee
and the requisite smile,
he sat cornered in this office at last
and crossed and uncrossed his legs
and asked if he could smoke
and said he didn't know about the money problem,
and I said, "It's your business
until you represent the company,"
and he said it was a misunderstanding,
and I asked about all the others,
and he said they were mistakes
and he would explain
and the company would not be liable,
and I said we'd heard it before.

He sucked the cigarette red and squinted
and said, "What do you want me to do?"
And I thought,
    Oh God, I want you to quit,
    to clear out, to take away this pain.
    I want you to stand, shake my hand,
    take early retirement, give it up,
    find a job, land on your feet,
    be happy. But I want you gone.
But I said, "What do you want to do?"
And he said, "I've been drinking a lot,"
and I wondered if he was lying about that too
And I said, "I know."

I FIND MYSELF WISHING

I find myself wishing I could be like Mr. Dithers
so I could jump up and dash down the hall
and into an office
and shout,
"Bumstead (or whatever the name is)
you blithering idiot, you're fired,
clean out your desk and be gone by five!"
What a luxury,
but it only happens in the comics.
There are the legalities, of course,
making the damned paper trail,
but that's not what stops me.
And it's not that firing someone
is, as the books say, my own failure.
No, I think it's knowing
that I will never be forgiven
even if I could apologize,
as in some cultures they apologize
to the game they are about to kill.
"Forgive me, please, I'm about to take your life.
You're fired."
Even that would be simpler than the real thing,
than now, sitting here,
waiting for the knock on my door.
Never mind the greater morality,
the justice of the group,
all those answers I know so well.
Let's bring it down to one and one,
a handshake,
some sentences,
what it takes to face the watering eyes,
the denial,
the disbelief,
the anger,
the fear,
the betrayal.

Understanding Honesty

Honesty is the best policy. Always. Honesty with your boss, honesty with your employees. and honesty with yourself. Need anyone say more on this subject?

Yes.

We need say more because there are plenty of managers who try to disguise a multitude of sins as honesty. One of the most successful entrepreneurs I know, a man of wealth and political influence and high community standing, seems proud of his reputation as one who is "blunt and to the point," as the newspapers describe him.

"I don't always make people happy," he is quoted as saying, "but I get my point across. Maybe I'm candid to a fault, but I find it saves time."

Ah yes, saves *time*, the irreplaceable commodity.

For years I've heard the same thing from a manager who is described by many as a "bulldog." Others describe him in ways not suitable for print.

Both men are knowledgeable and talented, but their technique of bludgeoning people with language in the name of honesty is at the sacrifice of effective management.

I do not claim that *they* are ineffective. To the contrary. But they could be even more effective if they would not let a distorted notion of honesty handicap their potential as leaders or managers.

The same is true of an advertising executive I know. Her consistent complaint is that no one on her staff has really good ideas, yet her way of evaluating ideas is to examine them aloud in groups, with her best evaluation being a grudging acceptance, and her worst being public ridicule, a scathing criticism in infinite and baroque detail of the idea's originator.

Of course, she'd argue that she ridicules no one; she is "just being honest." She would also say that her criticism is never of the person but of the idea. "All ideas must be able to stand rigorous examination," she says.

Of course. Be honest. Examine ideas and other work rigorously. That's also part of being a manager, of assuring the best work, of producing better products and services.

But too often, that's not what's really going on in these situations.

To begin with, in my experience the managers who use the most brutal language are themselves people who are extremely sensitive to criticism. They feel they shouldn't be criticized because they think of themselves as good people and good managers who are forced to be blunt in order to "get the job done."

Ah yes, *get the job done*. It's right up there with *saving time* and *rigorous examination*. All those come under the disguise of *being honest*.

But that disguise has little to do with the issues behind these catchphrases. The issues are:

Honesty versus tactlessness.

Efficiency versus brutality.

Getting the job done versus undermining the confidence of the people who are supposed to get the job done.

Rigorous examination versus humiliation.

Saving time versus saving relationships.

If managers are to be liberated from old notions of straw-boss, kick-ass, drill-sergeant management in order to achieve effective, enlightened management and, we hope, leadership, then we have to examine our management behavior in light of what we want our people to accomplish rather than how it protects our own egos.

In fact, it is *dis*honest to bludgeon people with tactlessness. The manager who does it is lying, to the people and to himself, because that manager is not so interested in being straightforward and honest, in saving time, or in getting the job done as in showing who's boss. (Read: proving to *oneself* who's boss.)

Companies no longer can afford ego-driven managers who don't know what honesty is and is not, thus managers who will never become leaders and whose effectiveness will always be limited by the amount of ill will and discontent they are destined to create.

RESISTING

There are days when the old ways seem easier.
To hell with consensus
and community building
and conflict resolution
and gentle persuasion.
Time to kick some ass,
turn some heads around,
get some action,
make this place move.
Time to stop asking questions
and give some orders.
Time to get things
ready for inspection.

It's an old urge,
the luxury of power,
the first temptation of bosshood,
and it comes like a bad temper
on a day when someone won't accept
the answer I gave,
and pushes again,
another five-minute meeting that eats up an hour,
another printout to prove a point not worth proving,
another ploy to protect someone's invisible turf,
another dance along that border
between debate and defiance.
I feel the anger flashing
and fight what I want to say,
all the top-sergeant stuff
like "Shape up or ship out,"
or "Tell it to the chaplain."
When I'm lucky,
the thought of those words
bouncing off the paneled walls
makes me smile.
When I'm not,
I take a very deep breath.

Overcoming the Fear of Trust

HERE'S THE problem: Employees do not feel trusted, because management dreams up dozens of ways to tell employees that they are not trusted. In turn, the employees do not trust management.

Don't get me wrong, the problem is not restricted to business. All of our institutions—the government, medicine and health care, the military, the educators, even the church—send constant signals of distrust. We have created a society in which individuals and groups regard one another with a growing suspicion that has made us less productive and more litigious.

Yet one of the values we honor most in people is their trustworthiness. In business, to which I herein restrict my attention, you can hear a lot of lip service given to trusting the employees. It is a nice thing to say, and from every objective point of view makes a lot of sense. Everyone wants to believe that if people are trusted to do their work, they will do their work.

And I do believe it, but believe me, trust is hard work and it's scary. Why? Because some people can't accept trust. Notice I did not say "can't be trusted" or "shouldn't be trusted." I said they can't accept trust.

It is tempting to let this fact overshadow another fact: The great majority of people accept trust and thrive on it.

So by the philosophy of managing for the good people, the most rewarding and productive attitude is to trust everyone. It is pragmatic as well, because not trusting people has no effect on those who can't accept trust but has a debilitating effect both on those who can—and also on you.

I recognize how difficult it is to convey trust amid the systems and structures of business, but this is all the more reason to concentrate management attention on it. No one could reasonably question the need to establish office hours and work rules and standards of performance, because it is critical that everyone understand the expectations of the workplace. On the other hand, I have found that it is not the systems, structures, and rules that really convey distrust, it is their *enforcement* by managers that does the damage.

It's the old story of managers who fancy that their job is police work rather than missionary work. They become so preoccupied with making sure their employees are not doing the wrong thing that they fail to recognize the right thing, which may be something *not* according to the rules.

You as manager must trust your employees to do their work. You must trust them almost beyond reason. You must take them at face value and let them know you believe what they say and you believe they will do what they say they'll do.

And don't worry about being called naive. Sometimes I think "naive" is the most feared label in business—worse even than incompetent. In my experience, when someone calls a manager "naive," he really means "too trusting" or, in my view, "not paranoid enough," as if you constantly must be watching over your shoulder or questioning your employees' motives.

What a terrible way to manage, and what a terrible way to live.

It is far better to spend your efforts being a mediator and interpreter between the company's systems, policies, and procedures and your employees. It is a necessary role in every company.

I believe that my employer, the Meredith Corporation, is among the best-run companies in America, but even we do some dumb things that communicate distrust. For instance, we have a computer-generated absence-monitoring system for our nonexempt employees. When someone misses a day, the absence is duly recorded and reported, coded as excused or not excused.

Now get this picture: Suppose one of our longtime employees has had an outstanding attendance record for several years. Believe me, no computer-generated system will compliment him or her on that achievement. (With luck, the boss will be paying enough attention to do it.) But let that employee miss a day, and the Big Brother computer is right there with the "incidence" report. How can that fine employee feel trusted in such a system?

This is a case of the system itself automatically sending the message "we don't trust you." There is only one saving grace: The messages come through the boss. My fervent hope is that most supervisors do as I do, and throw them away before they get to the employee.

Most companies have some system like this, along with monitors on office hours, expense reports, travel time, and on and on. If these systems are regarded by managers as a source of information for determining more efficient or economical ways to do things, then okay. But if the manager lets these systems become big sticks with which to harass employees, then he or she destroys any chance of communicating trust.

In my past twenty years of management, I have *never* reprimanded anyone about office hours, time off, the length of the lunch hour, vacation days, sick days, or any of that. I have never questioned whether someone should have returned earlier from a trip, should or should not have stayed in a certain hotel, should or should not have had an extravagant dinner. For that matter, I haven't even tried to define extravagant. And I've never checked the atlas to make sure the company was not overcharged on a mileage claim. But I know managers who have made careers out of worrying about all that trivia.

Surely, you may be wondering, there have been employees who have taken advantage of me. Of course, I'm sure there are. I don't know exactly who they are, but I suspect they are the employees whose work was substandard, who did not grow, who did not produce, and who communicated their lack of commitment in many ways more significant than cheating on expense reports or taking extra days off. And, I suspect, they are among the employees I've fired over the years.

And that's part of the point: The employees who cannot accept trust in meeting the basic standards of fair dealing with the company cannot accept trust in doing the job itself.

As for policies, they should be enabling devices. People must feel that they can do what seems right and best without fear of punishment for violating some policy.

Also, avoid a lot of procedures. Instead, set goals and guidelines about the probable ways to achieve the goals. It is the height of management arrogance to believe we can sit in our offices and dream up the best procedures to fit every circumstance.

And as another very important step in conveying your trust to employees, learn to delegate. If you've read any management literature, from the most elementary to the graduate-school stuff, you'll find a lot of emphasis on delegation. Then you hear about monitoring.

Everything the literature says is true, but let me tell you how it works most of the time.

The boss calls in a favored employee and delegates a project to him. It goes like this:

"Joe, I want to delegate this matter entirely to you. Please get it done by September first, and let me know how you're doing every Monday morning between now and then. And by all means, if you have questions or need help, let me know."

Sounds clean. The project was explained, a deadline was set, and intermediate progress monitoring points were established. Right out of the book.

But how many bosses have you known who will then stop by the office of the manager or call him in a few days later (before the appropriate Monday morning reporting time) and say something like, "Oh, say, Joe, how are you coming on that project?"

Translation: "I delegated that assignment to you, Joe, but of course I don't really trust you to do it, so I'm going to check on it every damned time I see you."

So reading and talking about delegation is not enough; you have to be brave enough to go all the way with it. Which leads to the fundamental point: A good delegator is usually a manager who has overcome the fear of trust and who conveys trust in every exchange with employees, not just through delegation.

And the manager who has overcome the fear of trust has taken a pivotal step in getting the best results the group can produce.

THE LETDOWN

All the management books say
keep your expectations to yourself,
Give your employees goals
but not expectations.
All the child-care books say
the same thing.
But who do they think they're kidding,
those experts?
Haven't they ever had a child with promise,
a kid they just knew would do
everything they did,
and more?
Haven't they ever seen themselves
in the face and walk and hustle
of a young seller or engineer or manager,
and haven't they thought to themselves,
That's it,
that's what I'm looking for,
that's who I need,
the next one for the next big job?
And haven't they overlooked
the small things,
the should-have-seen-it-coming signs
that meant wait,
not ready yet,
too soon, slow down, hang on.
And didn't they think,
This is my guy
and he can't fail because he's as good
as I was,
and I'll help him over the rough spots,
and besides,
sometimes it's sink or swim in this business

and you can't know if you're ready
until you're right in the thick of it?

And have they never waited too long
to throw out the lifeline,
left only to watch the sinking
of their expectations?

EXECUTIVE HEALTH

Something happens,
a dizziness when you stand up,
a pain you never noticed before,
a heavy breath at the top of the stairs.
And you think about a friend in the hospital,
and wonder what's going to get you someday.
So you make another vow,
you buy a diet book
and new workout clothes
and a computerized treadmill
and meditation tapes,
and you renew the health-club membership
and get your racquet out of the closet
and inflate the tires on the bike
and walk three miles the very first day.

Then it's Monday,
and the broiled fish you were going to have
turns into pasta
and the dessert you'll always skip
becomes just sherbet,
and out of the office by five
means still there at seven.
On Tuesday you can't work out on an airliner,
and who in his right mind jogs
after dark in a strange city?
And the tapes you play for stress
put you to sleep at the wrong time,
so you lie awake later,
listening to the horns and the garbage trucks
and the sound of your own breathing,
and vow to make another start this weekend.

Management's Insoluble Problem

WHILE LISTENING to the problems of a symphony conductor friend a few years ago, I said, "Sounds as if you have what we in business frequently call a personnel problem."

"No," he said. "For me, it's far more an *artistic* problem. There is a principal player who should be replaced, but he has something like tenure and I can't do it."

"Oh," I said. "So in my terms, is it a productivity problem or a quality problem?"

"It's both," he said.

He could have been speaking for any business manager, for he was talking about one of the most common and insoluable management problems, that of the *old pro*. In more generous and appropriate terms, it's the worker who has reached the level of performance he is capable of, or is interested in, reaching. Unfortunately, that level is not up to the current level of the rest of the group. I'm sure your company has a name for the syndrome.

A business friend who is also a pilot refers to it as "the glide pattern," and we all know someone who has gone into the glide pattern.

But the conductor's and the manager's problem is more complicated than someone simply getting lazy after some years in the job. As the conductor put it, "It's not that the player doesn't *want* to be better; he just doesn't have the ability. He is performing at his very best all the time. It's just not good enough."

"So what harm does it do?" I asked. "He plays his part as he always has, and things are okay, right?"

"But he limits the ensemble."

Aha, I thought. There's the rub for all of us.

"One of my responsibilities," said the conductor, "is to be challenging the musicians, to be increasing the level of performance, to always be improving the ensemble. Part of the way I do it is by expecting a higher standard, and another is by choosing programs that require a higher standard."

"Always making them reach a bit?"

"Exactly."

Again, he could have been speaking as a business manager.

On the one hand, we know there are strong performers and weak performers. Most company compensation systems, with their merit-increase ranges reflecting some kind of bell-curve expectation, attempt to reward according to an appraisal or rating system.

As with so many other systems, the compensation system fails to accommodate the ideal that the manager wants *everyone* to perform well, and that in this increasingly competitive world, a business's survival and growth may depend on better-than-average performance by everyone in the group.

So we recognize the people in the glide pattern by giving them lower-than-average merit increases for their lower-than-average work.

They aren't bad enough to fire, and they aren't good enough to provide any further growth. But understand this: These workers may be trying their best. They may be working hard and doing every bit as good a job as they did five years ago.

Of course, they may not, and that makes the manager's job all the more difficult, for the first thing to do is to evaluate to your satisfaction the *quality of the effort*. If you are satisfied that the quality of effort represents the employee's best possible work, then the problem can't be solved by training or by appraisal and counseling. You have to accept the worker as is.

But what happens to the ensemble? It suffers. The standard has changed because the rest of the group performs at a higher level, but the glide-path worker just keeps plugging along.

Consider a sales situation, for instance. Suppose a salesperson has been at it for twenty years and knows the accounts and all the people involved. Let's say he is a man and has, in his career, become what we might call a good journeyman salesman. Although he sells about the same volume he always did, the other salespeople in the department have been able to increase their volume by 10 percent for the past couple of years. As sales manager, you just know that if you could put a more energetic and vibrant personality into the job, you'd get more volume out of those accounts.

You review the accounts with the old pro; you monitor sales-call reports and letters; you know he is calling on the right people and he is telling the story as it should be told. Your analysis of the problem is unscientific but accurate: The clients just don't feel very motivated to buy more business from this salesman, although they like him just fine.

It happens all the time.

So do you fire him? Surely, a manager can't afford to manage to the lowest common denominator and must weed out those who can't keep up.

On the other hand, is it fair or just or ethical to fire someone who was hired to do a job at a certain level and who, through no fault of his own, finds the level raised? Of course not. It is these kinds of change-the-rules actions that have resulted in tougher employment laws and have often legally restricted business from doing things that would have been fully justified.

And you can't just wait for him to retire, because the plateaued-performer syndrome *is not a matter of age*. It can happen at any age, but it usually happens after several years of tenure in the same kind of job.

So what to do?

Most companies I know try all kinds of solutions, none of them very satisfactory. Some try the organizational approach, in which the old pros are put into a separate department doing "special assignments." It's okay if you can afford the extra payroll costs and if you can figure out a way the other employees don't end up resenting it and the old pros don't feel useless and shunted aside. In my experience, this "solution" just postpones the problem for someone else to solve later when it's even more difficult.

Another possibility is to assign a "helper," called whatever title you can come up with. In the case of our salesman, the manager could assign another person to cover some of the accounts, perhaps even paying both salespeople a commission on those accounts as a trade-off for more volume.

This one can work too if you can find a way to keep the original salesman from feeling intruded upon and get him to work as a mentor or senior-support person. And if you can afford the cost of double-covering a territory.

Another approach is for the sales manager to become personally involved, to make calls in the territory and generally bring high-level support.

Most other solutions are variations of the organizational or double-coverage attempts.

None of them is very satisfactory in that they all impose some constraint on the group and the operation. What companies need more than anything else are programs for renewal and retraining that accommodate horizontal movement for people who either are burned out in a job or have reached their potential in that job. Of course, the legal, as well as the ethical, problems inherent in plucking people from one place and moving them to another grow more complex every day.

As accustomed as I am to offering solutions in these essays, I confess I am stumped. There is no easily applicable solution for this one, except to be sure that you appraise honestly—it is unfair and dishonest to give good appraisals to that salesman when he's 10–20 percent behind everyone else—and reward appropriately.

I am not sanguine about the problems, and I realize there may come a point when, for the good of the group, you have to do *something*, even if it disappoints the particular employee, seems unjust, or creates legal risk. But I'll also say this: You may just have to live with this reality and do the best you can.

After all, I listened to my friend's orchestra for several years. It sounded fine. The critics wrote well of it.

It could just be that only a few musicians heard the problem and that it made no real difference to the product. Or on a more haunting note, it could be that when the difference becomes obvious, it's already too late.

What Managers Hide Behind

Despite what business schools would have you believe, there are no hard-and-fast rules for evaluating managers. It is a very personal process, and when I am asked for guidelines, I can point only to results, many of which are subjective, such as morale and a sense of the environment, and many of which are measurable, such as productivity and financial accomplishments.

All of these can be misleading, however, depending on the point in a manager's tenure at which the measurements or judgments are made.

I know that, in the long run, a manager's effectiveness will prove out one way or another, but as a senior manager, I can't wait until things turn sour. Instead, I pay a lot of attention to style and to *what the manager feels is important*. Both can be predictors of results, and both can become what I call the manager's hiding place.

Whether you call them that or not, you'll know them when you see them. The paradox is that there are often good reasons managers begin to embrace these ways of thinking and of doing things. What happens, however, is that some managers get so comfortable in their particular patterns that they overdo it. Watch out for these hiding places:

Democracy. Sounds benign if not generous, doesn't it? And who could criticize the manager for running a democratic operation? I could and do. While I believe strongly in consultative management through which employees are kept informed and are consulted about decisions concerning their well-being or their department's well-being, and while I believe in consensus, a business operation does not run well by majority vote. In fact, a manager's notion of "democracy" is most often the avoidance of decision-making and a refuge from the hard work of leading and managing.

Just as in society, the majority rarely defends the views of the minority, so in business the majority rarely will support the ideas of the minority. And frequently, the best ideas— for products, for procedures, for innovations of all kinds— come from that one person who, thinking about the problem alone, comes up with a solution no one else has thought of. Not only have the others not thought of it, the first instinct of the group is to reject it.

Here is where the manager's judgment must prevail. As Gifford Pinchot III, author of *Intrepreneuring*, says, most corporations have an "idea immune system," which if left unchecked will beat down any new idea that tries to make its way into the corporate body, because any new idea represents the threat of change.

The manager always should seek consensus, but understand also that consensus sometimes must come *after* a decision is made. In the new workplace, the manager must honor diversity and innovation and change, and must often rule against the majority in order to keep the business moving in an ever-moving world.

Autocracy. Wait. I just said that democracy is not the answer and that the manager must often make hard decisions against the will of the majority. Yes, but I didn't say the manager has to be an "I'm-the-boss-around-here" autocrat.

Autocracy comes in all forms, from the overbearing straw boss who will browbeat you into his point of view, to the sweetly stubborn closed-minded parent who will smile and nod but never really listen, to the try-and-find-me recluse who will tell you that "if there had just been the opportunity to get together on this, we could have discussed it before the decision was made."

The manager must make the decisions, but the employees deserve to be consulted even when the decision will not go their way. And they deserve to have the decisions explained.

They do not deserve to be told, "Here's the way I've decided it. Take it or leave it."

The Big Picture. You know these types. They are aloof, always up there somewhere in the clouds, examining the big picture that only they can understand. They can't be bothered with the details.

I know a manager of a large department who is lost in the big picture. He doesn't read the financials, leaving that to his budget person; he doesn't pay attention to all the personnel paperwork crossing his desk, delegating his signature to his executive secretary; he doesn't even read the company publications.

I've got news for him and the others who are hiding in the big picture. The big picture is like a jigsaw puzzle, and if you don't get familiar with all the pieces, turning them regularly with your own hands every which way to make them fit, you'll end up hiding in someone else's big picture and never creating your own.

All the paperwork and administrative detail is a pain in the neck, and I don't like it at all, but I know that the ebb and flow of an organization is revealed in the ebb and flow of the details. If you're paying attention, the big picture can become clearer with every piece of paper.

The Details. Okay, okay, I said that the big picture is full of details and you have to pay attention, but there *is* a limit.

I know a senior executive in my business who loves to say, quoting Mies van der Rohe, "God is in the details." And I always want to answer, "Yes, but not in the nit-shit details."

The details make a great hiding place, because you can always be at your desk, head down, busy busy busy, so preoccupied that your people are intimidated out of interrupting you. And you can take a big briefcase full of papers home every night, which impresses everyone, employees and senior management. Of course, if you need a hiding place from the bothers of family, the briefcase full of papers works almost as well as working late at the office.

The key to managing the details is in knowing which are important and will give you the information you really need, and which should be delegated or ignored. Understand also that while the details can keep you in touch with the ebb and flow of the operation, they can so engage you that you become disengaged from the most important part of the organization, the people.

They. You know who "they" are. They are the ones who write the policies that a manager can hide behind. They are the ones who run the bureaucracy that the manager can hide behind. They are the faceless powerful ones who the timid manager can invoke as the source of all unpopular decisions the manager "has" to make.

In other words, "they" are the company, the personnel department, the legal department, the tax department, the compensation department, the production department, the shipping department, the promotion department, and the purchasing department. Or if "they" can't be located inside the company, "they" abound on the outside. "They" are the competition, the marketplace, the consumers, the government regulators, the employment laws, inflation, recession, foreign investors, and on and on. In other words, "they" are any scapegoat the cowardly manager can blame his ineffectiveness on.

Personal Style. You've seen the busy-executive routine, I'm sure, the one in which every phone call, every letter, every meeting, is more important than the immediate matter at hand, and is particularly more important than dealing with, listening to, or caring about the employees.

Then there is Mr. Nice Guy who wants everyone to like him. And generally everyone does, but they don't respect him a lot because they can't get decisions. And that's because he can't make a decision without displeasing *someone*.

And don't leave out Mr. Tough Guy. He growls a lot but listens very little. He *will* make a decision, no pussyfooting around, and don't try to change his mind. He'll tell you what he *thinks* about everything, but you'll never know how he feels about anything. And when his decisions come out wrong, he blames his employees.

There are other hiding places, of course, but these are the ones I see most commonly used. If I find a manager engaging in any of these patterns of behavior, I try to help him or her make a change before the bad results begin.

If you wait for the bad results, you wait too long.

PART IV

THE COMMUNITY OF WORK

The Job Is the New Neighborhood

AND FRIENDS and co-workers are the new extended family.

We all know how the seeds were sown to produce these conditions of the new workplace: the statistics on mobility, the decline of the "traditional" family, and all that. But we in management have not yet paid enough attention to the new role that has emerged for business.

Some would say it has been this way always, that lifelong friendships and familylike bonds have been formed since people first were gathered in a "workplace." That has been true only as a manifestation among workers without the support of—and often despite the efforts of—management. Heretofore, management has very rarely concerned itself with creating an environment in which these connections were encouraged and nurtured. The attitude generally was whatever the employees wanted to do with *their* time was okay with management.

In the new workplace, the bonds of family and neighborhood have emerged so strongly that managers, running to catch up, may arrive to find an environment the employees already have created.

Take, for instance, the story of Mr. Randy Theis, as reported in 1989 in the *Des Moines Register*. Mr. Theis, an employee of the Des Moines Water Works, was stricken with cancer and was told by his doctors that he would be off the job six to ten weeks. But his surgery, which required ten-and-a-half hours, produced complications that pushed back his return-to-work date.

Mr. Theis, it should be noted, had five children under the age of fourteen. He'd had another cancer operation several months earlier, after which he used up all but two weeks of his sick leave and vacation.

As we know, this tragic situation is not uncommon in one variation or another, but would we expect the Des Moines Water Works to have some policy to allow more time for Mr. Theis? Of course not. Health-care costs already are outrageous and virtually out of control for most businesses.

It was one of those times when, clearly, management could do nothing without creating major problems of equity and, perhaps, legality.

But an unexpected and wonderful thing happened. Mr. Theis's fellow employees got together and came up with an idea: Each would *donate* time, that is, each would transfer vacation and personal-leave time to Mr. Theis so he could continue to feed his family during his recovery.

Consider that for a moment. The company would be out nothing, because those hours were already a part of overhead. All management had to do was somehow accommodate the transfer of time.

Naturally, the Des Moines Water Works had no policy allowing this kind of transfer, but to the credit of the utility's board of trustees, they created a policy. Twenty-five workers signed up to transfer time.

In addition, they organized a food drive for the family and collected money to help the children at Christmas.

Well, we can read heartwarming stories of one kind or another all over the place during the holiday season, but there's a difference with this one.

The difference is the lesson for management. We managers

must recognize that in this almost sudden, compulsive search for connection and a sense of community, business has an unprecedented opportunity to create a special place, which in the old days we thought of as just a place to work.

Despite rising costs, we must come to grips with issues of child care, parental leave, employment of the disabled, education and training of workers for fast-changing jobs, and accommodation of aging workers who do not want to retire.

We must come up with new ideas for self-management, for shared responsibility and authority, and shared ownership.

Jack Stack, president of Springfield Remanufacturing Corporation (SRC) has taken these concepts to their ultimate conclusion and has created a company that is owned by its employees, with Stack himself owning only 19 percent. He shares all information about the company, and all employees participate in management.

He told *Inc.* magazine that his system gives all employees a scorecard and a way to influence the score. "Besides," he is quoted as saying, "I was going to be leading the charge up the hill. I wanted to make sure that when I got to the top of the hill and turned around, there was a bunch of people coming with me."

In most public companies, we can't go as far as Stack did with SRC, but the companies who become more like SRC and pay attention to these concepts in the nineties will have a distinct competitive advantage in the quest for skilled, educated information and service workers.

So we managers have the opportunity to lead and direct people in that ever more powerful bond of common enterprise, and at the same time to create a place of friendship, deep personal connections, and neighborhood.

So how about this for a new management bumper sticker: IF YOU'RE NOT CREATING COMMUNITY, YOU'RE NOT MANAGING.

LISTENING AND LEARNING

There was a time I listened
to the men at the store,
thinking I could learn about farming
as they came dusty from the fields
in bib overalls and long-sleeved shirts,
their hands and faces dark red
save a white band where their straw hats sat.
They kicked their boots on the ground,
red clay dust rising to their knees,
and shook their heads as they came in the door.
Always shook their heads and met the eyes
of other farmers who shook their heads
and stood at the co-cola boxes
with a Coke or a Dr. Pepper or RC.
I listened about the weather
and the government
and the prices,
all of it turned against them.

Now, I watch businessmen
stretch and squeeze time on planes
and in offices,
measuring their days by meetings and phone calls,
then gather in clubs
and bars and restaurants
and shake their heads and talk and talk,
about inflation and disinflation,
about the government and the deficit
and the margins
and the share fights.

After a while, it sounds the same,
farmers and businessmen,
and what I hear
is how hard it is
for them to say how much they love it.

SELF-MADE?

He called himself a self-made man,
and his colleagues agreed.
"The kind of man who built this country,"
they said,
"Never asked anybody for help."
"Never took a dime he didn't earn."
"Made it on his own."
And so forth.

But can that really be,
the self-made somebody?
How many times do we ask for help
without ever using the words?
How much are we paid
before we're good enough to earn
the dimes we take?
And can we climb the ladder alone,
or do some of us just never notice
those lifts and boosts
along the way?

RECESSIONS

Why do we keep on keeping on,
in the midst of such pressure,
when business is no good for no reason,
when everything done right turns out wrong,
when the Fed does something
and interest rates do something
and somebody's notion of consumer confidence does
    something
and the dogs won't eat the dog food?

What keeps us working late at night
and going back every morning,
living on coffee and waiting for things to bottom out,
crunching numbers as if some answer
lay buried in a computer
and not out among the people who
suddenly and for no reason
are leaving their money in their pockets
and the products on the shelves?

Why don't we just say screw it
instead of trying again,
instead of meandering into somebody's office
with half an idea,
hoping he'll have the other half,
hoping what sometimes happens will happen,
that thing, that click, that moment
when two or three of us
gathered together or hanging out
get hit by something we've never tried
but know we can make work the first time?

Could that be it,
that we do all the dull stuff
just for those times

when a revelation rises among us
like something borning,
a new life, another hope,
like something not visible catching the sun,
like a prayer answered?

A Manager's Guide to the New Values

THE FIRST thing to remember is that there are no new values, just old values with new names.

But before giving you the list for easy reference, I offer some background.

To begin with, a quote from T. S. Eliot: "Half the harm that is done in this world is due to people who want to feel important." How true of business! Of course, it begs the question of what it means to feel important. In a way, everyone wants to feel important, but does that mean king of the hill or first among equals or, simply, a necessary member of the community?

Given that everyone wants to feel important, let's ask what that means to the new workers, the much-heralded baby boomers. These young people bring a curious mixture of conventional thinking and "New Age" ideas gleaned from their adolescent and teenage years in the sixties and seventies when many of them explored their own consciousness through everything from transcendental meditation to drugs to confrontation therapy to *est* to Zen. Even if they did not personally experience these things, many of today's "thirtysomething" workers understand what was going on then, and they aspire to many of the values that derived from those experiments.

In seeking "the right path," these young people establish goals that almost paradoxically embrace the material and the spiritual. Contrary to what most social prognosticators were predicting back in the halcyon days of emerging social consciousness, the baby boomers are most readily finding the magic mixture they seek in the arena of business.

In turn, they are bringing into business different ways of addressing values.

A baby-boomer friend, a former department head, used to start meetings that she knew were going to be difficult by saying, "Let's all proceed with the *presumption of goodwill*." Her notion of goodwill was driven by a fundamental belief in the goodness of most people, regardless of what their roles might occasionally impose upon them. She believed that, given a clear sense of shared goals, people will respond positively even when their responses may be in conflict with one another.

There was nothing new about the values underlying my friend's belief, but her articulation of them in the workplace was new. She left management a few years ago, but several of us still use her very effective "presumption of goodwill" phrase in tough meetings.

This little anecdote illustrates the most important thing about the changes now making their way into business: It is individual people who are reshaping the workplace, rather than institutional forces dictated by top management.

Marilyn Ferguson, author of *The Aquarian Conspiracy*, writes, "Throughout history, virtually all efforts to remake society began by altering its outward form and organization. It was assumed that a rational social structure could produce harmony by a system of rewards, punishments, manipulations of power. But the periodic attempts to achieve a just society of political experiments seem to have been thwarted by human contrariness."

Whether by human contrariness or simply because of the

difficulties of imposing bureaucratic systems on one of people's most spiritually necessary functions, *work*, business has suffered problems parallel with those of society.

But the good news is that business changes faster than the government and the society at large. Ms. Ferguson herself writes, "Business executives may be the most open-minded group in the society, far more open than scholars or professionals, because their success depends on being able to perceive early trends and new perspectives."

Which is why the baby boomers have been able to bring "new values" into the workplace; which is why management styles and techniques have been changing more rapidly than any other part of business.

This value-quest has produced, for the first time in the history of American publishing, a decade in which business books consistently have been on the best-seller list. And most of those books are dealing with values and relationships, not high finance.

Thus the manager's challenge at all levels is to be an agent of change and not just be swept along, sometimes kicking and screaming.

Which brings me to the list of old values and new values. But wait, I said there are no new values, only old ones with new names. True, but there are values upon which we traditionally have based much of management, and there are values that to this point have not found their way into conventional management thinking. To that extent, these values may be new to most managers.

I heard Ms. Ferguson present a similar comparison in a workshop, and have adapted the list for management. The "traditional" values are best called "protection" values, whereas the "new" ones are called "growth" values.

Protection Values	*Growth Values*
Safety	Spontaneity (risk, freedom)
Feeling superior to others	Feeling connected to others
Ego defenses	Vulnerability
Self-control	Self-knowledge

Protection Values	*Growth Values*
Knowledge (facts)	Wisdom (truth, ability to learn)
Role-playing	Authenticity (being the same wherever you are)
Comfort at all costs (avoid pain)	Truth at any cost (accept pain)
Control of others	Communication with others
Permanence	Potential

A close examination of this list reveals a paradox: The "new values" are much closer to what we think of as "traditional social values," those about which there is so much talk these days. "A return to traditional values," in business terms, may more properly be thought of as a reexpression of the values society has held most dear. The form of that reexpression in the workplace is as growth values.

Clearly, a manager who, in T. S. Eliot's terms, wants to feel important is driven by the protection values, the old values of the workplace. But there *is* the other way to feel important, to bring enormous worth and value to the manager role. And that is to realize, as Ms. Ferguson so aptly puts it:

"The past is not our potential."

Mixing Religion and Management

AFTER READING Robert Pirsig's wonderful *Zen and the Art of Motorcycle Maintenance* and John Heider's very useful little book *The Tao of Leadership*, I got to wondering what kind of a businessperson Jesus would be.

After all the attention given recently to Eastern spiritual disciplines, it seems appropriate in a country of so many professed Christians to consider Christian teachings in some pragmatic context not usually discussed by the theologians. And what context is more pragmatic than business?

There is one particular group that might say they've done it already. They call themselves "Christian businessmen," and they even have their own "Christian Yellow Pages." But I'm afraid some of them forgot to ask themselves the starting question: "What kind of a businessperson would Jesus be?"

Having been raised a fundamentalist Christian, I worry about what the Christian Yellow Pages are really saying. One clear inference is that the "other" Yellow Pages are non-Christian.

Which leads me to speculate that Jesus himself might not choose to advertise in the Christian Yellow Pages.

Wait. Don't accuse me of blasphemy before you read the Gospels again. And don't think Jesus wouldn't advertise. Jesus knew how to draw a crowd, and He knew how to get His story across in very few words, some of them clever and some of them straight.

And He didn't have anything against commerce—only against what people become in the pursuit of commerce. Remember also that he had a few stories about making money and storing up treasure.

Contrary to what I believed as a child, he didn't have anything against money changers either, but he had definite ideas regarding their presence in the temple. Yet even in the story of how he drove them out, his anger wasn't about money-changing being evil. It was about misusing temple space meant for other people, women and poor people mostly.

It was about how some businessmen thought they owned the temple and didn't leave room for others. It was about *exclusivity*, which, of course, is a lot of what the Christian Yellow Pages are about. And they are about persuading other Christians to spend their money with the Christian business-men. But there's nothing about how to bring Christian phi-losophy into business through management.

So when I think of Jesus as manager or Christian teachings in business, I don't think of the Christian Yellow Pages. I am more likely to think of Jan Carlzon, the CEO of Scandinavian Airlines, who turned his company around by "turning the organization chart upside down."

Mr. Carlzon realized that the people at the "bottom" are the ones creating his daily "moments of truth."

Think about it. This is a very Christian concept, making the people at the "top" the servants of the people at the "bot-tom," honoring them, seeing to their welfare, recognizing their work as the vital work.

Or I might think of Barry Flint, who served as executive director of the Institute for the Advancement of Health. In talking about confrontations with employees, he said, "There comes a point at which I have to give them their humanity. Fundamentally, though, each person—things being equal—

knows what's good for him or her to do. If I'm honest and don't play games, I know things will be okay."

There are popular books about renewal, about empowerment, about love, in the workplace. I believe that what all of them address, in one way or another, is a workplace better than the one most of us have now. It is a workplace where there are people of goodwill, who listen to one another, who are not given to arguing, but who feel free to express differing viewpoints.

It is a workplace with a management sensitive to the weaknesses as well as to the strengths of the people and the business; a management that gives everyone special treatment; a management that concentrates on the working environment and that realizes that *the process of doing business is the most important part of business.*

And in this workplace, everyone is treated with dignity and respect, with honesty and trust, and with love—the values and qualities that will make business better even when business is not going so well.

I think that's the kind of business Jesus would run. We could call it Christian business; we could call it humanistic business; we could call it smart business.

Whatever we call it, sounds like heaven to me.

The Elements of
Enrichment

I'M WITH those psychologists who say that an enriched environment helps stimulate enriched thinking. In business, that means a workplace that is deliberately and carefully enriched for the employees will result in an increase in the "it-ies": creativity, quality, and productivity.

The enrichment can take many forms, and what you do to effect a richer environment depends on what you're doing now. Some places are richer than others.

About twelve years ago, Meredith Corporation management in Des Moines decided to completely recycle the old corporate headquarters. It was a mess of a building, added onto twice over the years, with a basement and subbasement that were originally designed to accommodate typesetting, engraving, and printing facilities, although those functions had moved to their own plant twenty years earlier.

The remodeling process itself was planned to disrupt business activities as little as possible. Still, it was awful: dusty, smelly, noisy. But little by little, as one area and then another was opened up, the positive effect on morale was palpable. Then, when the entire building was done, inside and out, including soaring entryways, murals, plants, restrooms with clouds on the ceiling, art on the walls, and sunlight and color everywhere, the place was opened for public tours.

The CEO in his wisdom invited the rest of the business community to come see what "we" had done.

No, we can't calculate the ROI, and we can't measure morale by the numbers, but it soared like the entryways, and so did productivity.

That's an example of enriching the physical environment.

More important is the psychological and emotional environment, the enrichment of which once again depends on what you're already doing.

I try to do it in many ways, and in different ways depending on the employee group.

For instance, the Meredith editors and designers in Des Moines often feel that they are not exposed to the creative stimulation available to their counterparts in New York. Never mind that most of the time, their counterparts either are not exposed to it or are not taking advantage of it. The perception in Des Moines is that everyone in New York spends all leisure time at lectures, galleries, shows, and such. Not only that, the New Yorkers are exposed to "top names" in our business and others.

What to do? Should I have tried to convince the Des Moines creative group that the New Yorkers don't get all that "exposed" either, thus trying to change the perception?

Well, you don't need a Ph.D. in psychology to know that wouldn't work. Besides, I couldn't deny that there was *some* truth to the perception that opportunity for creative stimulation is not as available in Des Moines as in New York.

The first thing I tried years ago was a "feed your eyes day." As editor in chief of *Better Homes and Gardens*, I suggested that when an editor or designer had an assignment in some city, he or she take an extra day to feed the eyeballs—museums, galleries, shows, and so on.

Then we tried a film series. We brought in films from all over the world and showed them free in a conference room. In the past few years, we've taken a more direct approach.

We carved out a budget for bringing in speakers to our corporate headquarters in Des Moines. The budget was to pay for honoraria and expenses, and there were to be no criteria set by management and no restrictions. Administration of the funds and selection of the speakers were strictly up to a volunteer committee made up of members of the creative group.

In the several years this program has been in place, the group has heard such speakers as Daniel Schorr, the broadcaster; Ralph Nader, consumer activist; Linda Ellerbee, broadcaster and columnist; Dr. Betty Sue Flowers, professor of English at the University of Texas, expert on mythology, and editor of the book *Joseph Campbell and the Power of Myth*; Michael Gartner, president of NBC News; Doug Greene, entrepreneurial publisher and "New Age" businessman; Doug Kruschke, president of Insynergy, a consulting and training business for high-level managers who are trying to bring new values into business; Paul Koestenbaum, philosopher and consultant to large corporations on "philosophy and business"; Milton Glaser, the designer; and many managers within our own corporation.

Attendance is voluntary, and those who choose to attend are given time off from work to do so.

The results are impossible to quantify, but when a member of the creative group tells me about what a great opportunity it is—and I hear it several times after each presentation—I know all I need to know. It's working.

Several years ago, I escorted all the *Better Homes and Gardens* Test Kitchen home economists to New York for a tour of restaurants and food markets. The objective was to broaden their understanding of food and food preparation outside the home kitchen. The restaurateurs and merchants were wonderfully responsive, giving the home economists special treatment everywhere. The trip brought significant change.

But enrichments don't have to be that elaborate or expensive. A party can work wonders.

I encourage celebrations of all kinds: promotions, a breakthrough sale, a new account, a record-breaking month; or on the more personal level, an engagement or marriage, a new baby, a service anniversary, even a birthday.

So you lose twenty minutes while everyone gathers for snacks and refreshments, silly speeches, and some conversation. So what? I say grab on to every opportunity to demonstrate that joy and celebration are part of the work experience.

And every once in a while, the timing depending on your business, spend more money and send some successful operation—even a small department that has exceeded its production or cost-control goals—away to a nice place for a conference. Sales groups are accustomed to conferences, but in my experience a special meeting out of the office can work wonders in a department not accustomed to such treatment.

It doesn't have to be Hawaii; in fact, it doesn't even have to be out of town. In the Meredith Magazine Group, some departments go to a local hotel, rent a conference room, have lunch, spend the afternoon in workshops, have a reception and dinner, then go home and come to the office the next day. When the weather is nice, a group may spend a day at a state park.

Nothing elaborate about that, but you would be amazed at the enriched creativity and thinking such a day produces.

In these days of "lean and mean" management, such spending may seem like fat to be cut rather than part of the true muscle of the operation. But take my word for it, you'll spend a lot of money on things that won't come close to a conference in its morale and productivity ROI.

Finally, the greatest job enrichment of all is your attitude. If you will pay attention, listen, be accessible, open up, and provide your people with as many special treatments and celebrations and learning experiences as you can, you'll be overwhelmed by the abundance of rich thinking all around you.

HOW IT WAS

They'll never know how it was,
the younger guys,
to bust our asses for a six-hundred-dollar raise
and a title change
and twice as much work.
They'll never bring lunch in a brown bag
or sneak to Lemo's
for a frosty beer when it was ninety-five degrees,
and the cheap bastards wouldn't spring
for air-conditioning,
and our pants stuck to the chair
and we thought we should get paid
for extra dry-cleaning.

Now everything is easy,
and they'll never understand,
the younger guys,
about changing things
and how long it took
to wait the old guys out.

James A. Autry

RETIREMENT PARTY

They all come,
even the ones who think
he was a pain in the neck.
They come and talk
about how he will be missed,
most of them never noticing he was there.
They come for themselves,
like going to a funeral
out of the fear of being buried alone someday.

They line up for coffee
and punch and cookies,
there being no official alcohol on the premises.
They read telegrams from old customers and old
    vendors
and old office buddies long retired.
They give him the right gift,
the rod and reel
or the camp stove
or the camera
or the round-trip ticket to somewhere,
bought with the fives and ones and quarters
from the manila envelope that has
in his last month
made its way all around the company.

He is moved by the attention,
by the feeling he is loved
and will be missed
and things won't be the same without him,
and he says some words
about how he will never forget any of them.
He introduces his family, who came halfway across
    the country
just for the occasion,
then everybody drifts toward their offices
saying good-bye with things like

"You lucky bastard,"
and "You don't even have to get up tomorrow,"
and "Stay in touch,"
and "Come visit,"
and other words of comfort for times like these.

How to Recognize the Heroes

THE HEROES of business are everywhere, but you won't necessarily read about them in *The Wall Street Journal* or *Fortune* or *Forbes*, and you won't necessarily find their books on the best-seller lists or their faces in the ads for for their companies.

There are heroes in the executive offices and boardrooms, to be sure, but most of the heroes of business never make it out of their own departments. And that creates a special challenge for managers: how to identify, then recognize and reward, the heroes.

Part of the process starts with knowing what to look for. I do this by dividing the heroes into three general types. The first is the *brave hero*.

There is a young woman in our customer service department who, taking matters into her own hands, made brave personal efforts to respond to a dissatisfied customer. What made her actions extraordinary is that she went against normal procedures and policies to do what she felt was right.

It was the sort of small act to which we give a lot of management lip service, but with which we aren't really comfortable. The problem was simple, a matter of a customer having been sent two bills because she had inadvertently ordered the same thing twice. The customer's error was obvious, and could be quickly spotted on the CRT screen.

But our procedure at the time was, if we received two orders, we sent two bills, even after the customer complained. For some reason having to do with procedural convenience rather than customer service, we required another notice from the customer in order to correct the error. Dumb.

And our customer service person thought so too. So she did something about it. Unfortunately, at the time she thought she might get in trouble for it.

That's the hero part. Heroes have to be fearless, which does not mean acting *without* fear but acting *beyond* fear.

But the heroes of a company are not just fearless about getting in trouble for doing the wrong thing. They are also fearless about doing something different, not usually done, outside the conventional wisdoms. These are the *crazy heroes*, the innovators, the ones you should give your eyeteeth for, but they are also the ones who often irritate the hell out of their supervisors.

George Bernard Shaw could have been writing about crazy heroes when he said, "The reasonable man adapts himself to the world; the unreasonable one persists in trying to adapt the world to himself. Therefore all progress depends on the unreasonable man."

One of the crazy heroes in our company is an advertising salesperson, a former rock-and-roll drummer who started in our company as a courier, driving the company van. Part of his job was to greet company visitors at the airport. After a while, it became clear that he had a special knack for public relations. Then he came to me and wanted to go into training as an advertising salesman. I agreed. We taught him all the tried-and-true things he should do, and when he learned those, he began to improvise.

He probably violates somebody's rules every day. He calls right at the top of a company and somehow makes friends with high-level people. He sends cartoons. He quizzes his customers about their knowledge of rock and roll.

He has been criticized, but those criticisms do not deter him from his own unique style. He has had problems from time to time, and he has to try hard to learn what works and what doesn't work, but he's still out there giving it his best. A crazy hero.

Then there are the heroes who are fearless in the amount of work they will commit to do. The *always-bite-off-more-than-they-can-chew heroes*. What makes them heroes, of course, is that they always seem to be able to chew and digest it all.

I have a lot of those in my group. There are art directors and production people who regularly go to the printing plant at 2:00 A.M. after working all day and before working the next day, just to make sure the reproduction quality meets our standards (which, of course, is just another way of saying it meets *their* personal standards).

There are circulation people who are sweating over models and analyses late into the evening and on the weekends, and financial people who will worry a problem through their PCs all night long, if need be, to find a solution.

Recently, two editors in our Special Interest Publications Group took on two completely new magazines at the same time they were doing their regularly scheduled publications, just to get them out in time for a special holiday-season effort.

Of my three kinds of heroes, the latter are easiest to spot, but all are vital to the growth and development and productivity of a company.

I believe that all companies have these heroes, because I believe it is in the nature of people to be heroes, given a chance. I believe people want to do what they think is right despite the rules, want to do things better despite the notion that they've never been done that way before, and want to work to their own capacities despite the "normal" expected standards.

The good manager has to be alert to the heroes and has to figure out ways of recognition and reward. Nothing huge is required.

I have a modest "Excellence Awards" program, modeled after one at Armstrong World Industries, Inc. It's simple.

There are three levels: awards given by department heads, awards given by group vice presidents and awards given by me, the group president. A recipient of the department-head award receives $100 (grossed up to be a net-after-taxes payment) and a small plaque. For the vice-president's award, we give $250 grossed up, plus a plaque. And for the president's award, we give $2,500 grossed up, plus an engraved silver bowl.

I press our managers to give a lot of department-head awards. Each vice president is allowed four awards a year, and I am trying for four or so president's awards a year. Each award recipient is mentioned in the company publication, and there usually is a coffee-and-presentation ceremony.

It ain't fancy, but it serves to let people know that we notice, that we appreciate what they're doing, that we care, and that we are willing to make a tangible recognition of the effort, even if the dollar amount may be modest.

It works. One of those editors who did all the extra work wrote me a note after sharing a president's award with a fellow editor: ". . . I feel crowned with the mark of excellence forever. There's a responsibility there, too. I will always respond—to the best of my ability. Your excellence program is very important and well-received." Spoken like a true hero.

Please understand that this program does not *create* heroes. They create themselves, and, believe me, there are plenty around, right in your own company. Look for them.

Managing Diversity

I SPENT several years of my career as head of a creative group of about 150 editors, writers, designers, and illustrators. During this period, one of my associates from a more traditional business part of the company used to call me the zookeeper.

It wasn't so funny, but we laughed anyway. Now, as companies embrace a more diverse workforce, some through government-imposed necessity and some through positively motivated initiative, I find I may have the last laugh. If those years on the creative side of our business taught me anything, they taught me about managing diversity.

It is one thing to honor diversity, to appreciate and respect the talents and character and values of people from all conditions of life regardless of age, gender, race, religion, sexual preference, or disability; it is quite another to manage that diversity.

If extreme situations can help make the point, I start with these from my own experience.

Several years ago, a woman came to me. "I have a confession," she said.

"Are you sure you want to tell me and not a counselor?"

I asked. This is always a good first reply to an oncoming confession, because there are a lot of things you as a manager should not want to hear. Always give the person a chance to back out.

"Yes," she said. "I have to tell you, because you'll be the first to notice."

I said nothing.

She looked furtively toward my door, then rose and shut it. I braced myself because, having worked with her for several years, I knew something weird was coming.

"I've cast a spell on the art director," she stage-whispered.

I then resorted to another ploy, which is more useful than you might think: I laughed.

Then I said, "What kind of spell?"

"I don't know exactly, but last night at midnight I went to his office and burned some incense and cast a spell to get him off my neck."

I knew that she and the art director had perennial problems with their separate views of how stories should be illustrated and what props should be used in photographs. Normal problems in a creative group. I knew also that she claimed to be descended from a witch and even to have a haunted painting hanging in her apartment. And she had named her cat Beelzebub. But this event seemed to be going too far.

How to handle it? In the need to honor diversity, must I never ridicule it? This situation on the face of it was ridiculous. Yet somehow I thought she was expecting that reaction and had chosen this technique, consciously or unconsciously, to focus my attention on her problems with the art director. I decided that my proper approach was to treat this eccentricity with as much seriousness as she did. Over the years since, it has always proved a valuable rule to treat any situation with as much seriousness as that felt by the people involved in the situation.

So I said, "Well, I just can't allow this. I can't have an art director under some sort of spell. You'll have to remove it, and we'll figure out some other way to get him off your neck."

She was relieved. She promised to remove the spell, although I can't vow that she did. And I kept my promise to be more responsive and more present in mediating differences between her and the art director (among others).

Then there was the man who invented and constructed various kinds of musical instruments, all of which looked like the sculpture they were intended to be but which *sounded* terrible. The problem was that he occasionally tried to play one during the day. I let his peers and colleagues deal with that one.

And one Thursday in the spring, one of the freer spirits came to the office with her legs painted in various colors and designs. This was in the miniskirt days, so her color statement had its intended effect. Her explanation was that "Thursdays are not as colorful as they should be."

Not all the situations arising out of diversity are funny or colorful, however. One of my more difficult management problems resulted from an out-of-the-office love affair that made its way into the office.

One of our women employees had a love relationship with a man in another city. Then word came that he was going to move to our city, to be with her and, at some point, to marry her. So far, so good.

A few months later, her manager came to me with the story of a love triangle. It seems that one of the woman's co-workers had met her fiancé and had fallen in love with him. The feeling was reciprocated, and the triangle began.

The basic situation is not rare, I suspect, but in this case the two employees sat side by side in the same department and often had to work together and in support of one another. Sticky. The further complication was that her co-worker was a man, so the relationship had both heterosexual and homosexual aspects.

Throughout all this, I felt it was important to focus my attention as a manager on the problems *in the office*. Nothing about the personal relationship was within any proper realm of management to consider, except the relationship between the co-workers.

At the time, I joked to our personnel director, "Look this

one up in your personnel manual and tell me what I'm supposed to do."

As complicated as this situation sounds, the solution was simple. I had the department manager call in the two and tell them that one of them was leaving the department. I left it to the manager as to how to make the decision. She could keep the one who was most talented and productive, or she could draw straws.

The ending is not dramatic. The manager made the decision. Fortunately, we had a job available in another department and were able to place the other employee. We told them to keep their conflict out of the office, and there would be no further problems.

A few months later, one of them resigned, but to this day I do not know who ended up lovers with whom. Nor should I.

The humorous and sad anecdotes I've shared here are all about white Anglo-Saxon people. No people of color. No disabled people. No "ethnics." The point this makes, I believe, regardless of the fact that these stories are about so-called creative people, is that people need not have obvious differences to be unique. We in management have kidded ourselves for years with the illusion that people are alike just because they look alike and dress alike and live in similar houses and belong to similar clubs. Everyone is unique, regardless of outward appearances.

What we must realize is that honoring diversity in all forms is in the near future of all American companies. We need the talents and productivity of every good worker if we are to succeed in a diverse and challenging marketplace.

ROMANTIC REVELATIONS

My friend has an infallible rule
for spotting a romance in the office,
a rule true and proven over the years,
accurate in direct proportion
to how hard the lovers try to hide.
My friend calls it the Law of Romantic Revelation,
and it goes like this:
    If you think they're doing it,
     they're doing it.
Sounds silly but it's damn near perfect
if you have any power of observation at all.
If for instance a very solid citizen,
say a forty-five-year-old guy,
stops getting a haircut every other week,
and as the hair begins to hide his ears and collar,
you notice the gray ones are gone,
or if he shows up in an Italian blazer,
unvented,
with notched lapels,
watch out.
Next thing you know he's collecting wine
or original prints.
Then one day you're in a meeting
on personnel policy
and find he has become a feminist
since the last meeting,
or you notice in the corner of his office
a new Land's End canvas bag
for his running shoes and designer sweats
and one of those Fit at Fifty
posters on the wall.
You have but to keep your eyes open
and the object of his affections
will come into focus
and the Law of Romantic Revelation
will unveil its infallibility once again.

Laws and Opportunities

I REMEMBER a top executive, a close acquaintance, railing against the government one day several years ago. It was after the Vocational Rehabilitation Act was passed, in which Section 504 required that public enterprises, including businesses, accommodate the disabled by providing ramps and elevators.

My colleague was cursing government interference that causes burdensome costs for business.

"We have to spend thousands of dollars to accommodate perhaps twenty people a year who are in wheelchairs," he said. "It doesn't make sense. It's just more bureaucracy at work."

The strange thing about my executive acquaintance's attitude is that he is severely hearing-impaired in one ear. He must position himself carefully at meetings or lunches or he will not be able to hear much of the proceedings.

When he was complaining about Section 504, I decided, at the risk of offending him, to stand on his hearing-impaired side and talk to him. "We're all disabled in some way," I said in a normal tone of voice.

He turned his head sharply. "What did you say?" he asked. "You're on my deaf side."

"I was just pulling your leg and making a point," I said, then told him we are all disabled in some way.

He had enough sense of irony to laugh, but somehow he felt his disability was "different."

All our disabilities are different, of course, but they aren't unique. Someone else shares the disability specifically, and many people accommodate, even unconsciously, other people's disabilities.

Yet while most of us may accommodate and support our disabled friends and family, we somehow have trouble bringing that same attitude into the workplace.

By the time this book is published, I believe Congress will have passed the Americans with Disabilities Act. At this point (fall of 1989), many businesspeople are opposed to the legislation because of its "burdensome cost." Different song, same verse.

The history of these governmental initiatives, from the civil-rights legislation in 1964 to the EEOC laws to the Vocational Rehabilitation Act, has been that the majority of business executives *institutionally* oppose the presumed negative impact on business. Then the legislation passes. Next we wait for the executive branch to promulgate the "rules" for compliance. Next we wait to see how strict the enforcement will be, seeking legal advice along the way, meanwhile lobbying the agencies to make sure government realizes the cost impact. Then, as the shape of the rules and the enforcement come into focus, business complies. Sometimes grudgingly, sometimes willingly, depending on the business and the people managing it.

When the grudging businesses do their maneuvers to circumvent the law, the lawsuits begin. Individual workers use the laws to intervene on their own behalf. And yes, *some* of those workers and their lawyers use the laws in greedy ways, knowing that juries generally will find against a business, particularly a large one. Then we in business decry our litigious society.

And so it goes.

There is, of course, another way, and while it may be too late in some areas, it is not too late to avoid all this craziness upon the passage of the Americans with Disabilities Act.

We start with a basic, honest admission: If we in business had done the things we ought to have done—in carefully employing, honestly appraising, equitably rewarding, and compassionately firing employees as appropriate to the situation—we probably would have avoided all these intrusive laws to begin with.

This is not a matter of politics, partisan or otherwise. It is true that government often swings the pendulum too far. It is true that there is a tyranny in some bureaucratic treatment of business and businesspeople. It is true that elected officials often make business the scapegoats for what actually is a failure of public policy. But all this simply makes my point even stronger: Do it well from the beginning, and avoid the problems that beg government intervention.

By "Do it well," I mean do it with a sense that what is important to the community at large is ultimately important to business. If it is important to the community at large that all people be treated with dignity and be given a chance to be productive, it is important to business. After all, it does not require a Phi Beta Kappa in economics to know that, at some level, everyone is a customer, and the more affluent the community of customers, the better for business.

I realize that this is not an attitude that will drive the stock price quickly upward, but let us remember how recently women and people of color were *completely* outside the mainstream of business life. And look what they've contributed and how they've changed business in the past two decades!

With the right approach, we won't have to struggle that many years for disabled people to bring their own enrichment to the workplace just as other groups have done.

All it takes is for managers to realize that a great resource for growth and productivity is about to be brought more forcibly into the workplace. Whether we use that resource or not is just a matter of attitude.

I had dinner recently with the CEO of one of America's large and respected financial-services companies. I knew he had been involved in some local initiatives to employ disabled people, so I asked him how it was going.

"It's amazing," he said, "how our 'normal' employees have reacted to the disabled ones. The atmosphere seems to have softened somehow."

"What do you mean by softened?" I asked.

"It is as if everyone feels closer. Like a greater sense of community."

"And have you noticed any problems? Anyone resent the presence of disabled people or feel that they are somehow getting special favors? Is there any slowdown in work?"

"To the contrary," he said. "To begin with, we don't give the disabled special treatment except for accommodating them physically in small ways. We've made relatively small investments in equipment, but it's also true that we buy some kinds of equipment for everyone. It seems to me that productivity is better, if anything. Of course, I can't prove it yet."

And, of course, no one will ask him to prove it—only that the business wasn't *penalized* somehow by employing the disabled.

The overriding point is not the employment of the disabled, however. The point has to do with recognizing business opportunities—what most of us in management are paid to do—before the government shoves them down our throats.

Hiring disabled people—and others traditionally considered unemployable or minimally employable—provides business with four big opportunities: 1. To acquire long-term and committed employees who need and want a job and who need and want to do good work; 2. To help people gain dignity and income from a job, thus lessening the social-service burden (which so many businesspeople also grumble about); 3. To help create disposable income for people, thus creating more potential customers for business; and 4. To learn even more about all parts of the community that provides the basic environment in which business exists.

A lot of the hot business literature these days talks about visionary managers who are always looking for a chance to bring a "win-win" solution to business problems. If you're one of those visionary managers, here's your chance.

A HOMELESS POEM

I don't want to hear any of those poems
about how we are all homeless,
drifting on this planet, alone
in a cold and dark universe.
Baloney.
I want to hear a poem
about how some of us are homeless
and we step over and around them
and wish somebody would do something
that wouldn't raise taxes.
I want to hear a poem about
children in an abandoned car
scared in the night
that what has happened will happen again.
I want to hear a poem
about nice neighborhoods up in arms
because squatters have moved into the park
and are shitting under the shrubbery.
Spare me those lines
about how alienated we are,
how powerless,
how apart and how isolated;
spare me please all those phrases
of comparative misery
we use at cocktail parties
on the way to the therapist.
Write me instead a stanza of despair.
Make me feel the pain
when a baby's mother breaks its legs
and thinks she's only playing.
Make me vomit at the thought
of what a child has to eat.
Fill me with that insane warmth
an infant feels sucking milk
from an addict mother's breast.

And make my head roar
with the screams and sobs and moans
rising from the streets
and storefronts and overpasses
and bridges and park benches and slum rubble
and garbage dumps and junkyards
all over this land of plenty.

The Symbols of Bosshood

Everyone knows who the boss is, right?

He's the one with the big office in the corner, the office with the carpeting and the sofa and the bar and the paintings and the exercycle. He's the one with the sacred parking space and the private washroom and his own dining room. He's the one with the limo and the Lear jet. And when there's no company plane, he's the one who gets to fly first class.

All that and a big salary too.

In the military, the boss is even easier to spot: He has special insignia on his shoulders, an eagle or a few stars. And he usually has some young lieutenant with a notepad close at his elbow.

Accoutrements of power and authority have permeated organizations throughout history, either as symbols of honor for the leader or so everyone could recognize the boss.

But now we in business need to ask ourselves why we continue to create special customs and symbols for the top leaders. Surely not to tell who the boss is. Why, then?

The time has come for executive perks to be reevaluated in most businesses, and the evaluation should be solely on the basis of what the perks do for the company and the goals of the organization—not what they do to glorify the bosses.

I believe that top executives must be compensated well, in keeping with the risks and responsibilities of their jobs. Sometimes part of that compensation comes in the form of "perks," but it's time to separate the compensation-competitive perks from those that simply aggrandize the executive and make everybody else mad.

I believe in perks commensurate with the risk of a job, such as insurance policies, or estate-planning help, or income-tax preparation.

As for the others—parking places, big offices (yes, I have one), special dining rooms, executive washrooms, and the rest—they should be evaluated by one question only: Do they serve to move the business forward?

By moving the business forward, I also include anything that will lower the stress level or save the time of an executive. Consider the question of a company plane, for instance. Our company has two Lear jets. I fly on them regularly. I know that their principal role is saving time and making possible a much more tightly packed schedule than would otherwise be possible. In effect, they do move the business forward.

But these planes are *never* used for personal travel, and their use is tightly controlled and accounted for. Were they used simply for the personal convenience of company officers, then they would not meet the test of a business tool versus a perk.

There are probably good reasons, at one time or another, for private dining facilities. To save time. To entertain special customers. On the other hand, if the private dining keeps the boss away from the company cafeteria on a regular basis, then the dining room probably is hurting the business because it's keeping the boss from using a great keeping-in-touch resource.

I do not believe any of the other obvious perks—private planes for personal use, luxury cars, parking places, lavish offices, separate washrooms—meet the criteria of moving the business forward. In fact, I believe they create more resentment than they are worth.

I have heard top company executives laud the "inspiration" value of perks, saying that it gives young employees something to "set their sights on."

To the contrary, I believe the pattern of how an employee regards the boss's perks goes like this: To a young worker, the perks represent part of the reward of success and, as such, become part of the employee's own material goals. As time goes on and the perks seem farther away, they become a reminder of how far away from that success the worker still is.

Then, one day, the employee is walking in from the back parking lot, through the snow, in zero-degree temperatures, and, just before entering the building, sees one of the bosses pull his car into that sacred parking place, and it happens. The employee thinks, Why doesn't the son of a bitch have to find a parking place like the rest of us?

When that happens, the executive parking lot has just moved the business backward, because the resentment of corporate elitism has struck its blow.

Fact is, there are some employees who aspire to all the window dressing of the big jobs, but those probably are the employees who are focused on the job and not the work (see The Job and the Work, page 46). In my experience, those are not the employees most likely to move the business forward.

So if we are to establish a community of work in a company, an endeavor whose success depends on commitment by everyone, then everyone needs to feel special and needs to feel recognition.

This is difficult to begin with, but it is made especially difficult by setting up the kind of obvious caste system represented by frothy, brass-on-the-shoulder, elitist perks.

Better to set up a meritocracy in which all forms of recognition are suited to the effort of the individual and the group at all levels and in which compensation is appropriate to the responsibility and risk contribution of the job to the overall objectives of the enterprise.

In other words, equal recognition for good work, competitive compensation for the scope of the position, and no show-off perks.

DIALOGUE WITH THE PAST

What are you doing here
in this conference room,
out of the cotton fields and red dust,
looking over the coffee and pads
lined yellow and legal size,
pretending to be a company man?
What do you expect me to think,
with your country-church and preacher-man
   rightness,
nodding at the plan,
smiling at the chart,
acting like the profit margins make a damn
when I know where you come from?
Who do you think you're kidding,
the cowshit just off your shoes,
not far enough from overalls
to be happy in a collar,
with *GQ* in the briefcase,
a charge at Saks,
and your grandfather restless in the cemetery
every time your closet opens?

    Wait wait,
    I'm the same and it is too,
    and nothing changes but the words.
    When the CEO shuffles his feet
    in their Italian leather loafers
    and calls for further study
    and appoints a task force,
    it's one of the county supervisors
    in overalls and brogans
    kicking the dust and saying,
    "Well, fellers, sometimes I think, well,
    then again, I just don't know."
    And everybody goes off and thinks about it some more.

But what are you trying to prove
when you didn't have a pot to pee in
or a window to throw it out of,
when the roof leaked and the rats came in,
and you looking now to shelter
your money as well as yourself?

> *Only that I still want what I wanted*
> *when you cut through the shit—*
> *to do, to get, to hang on to something,*
> *and I only made the trade,*
> *country church for conference room,*
> *deacons for directors,*
> *and chicken in the pot for a few shares of stock.*

Managing Conflict

First understand that conflict is not bad and it is not destructive. Then understand that conflict is not good and it is not constructive. Then accept that conflict becomes good or bad to the extent that it either becomes growth and learning or hostility and failure. You as manager determine which it is to be.

A lot of managers think a workplace without conflict is a better workplace. Somewhat more comfortable for some people, perhaps, but not better. I think a workplace without conflict is a workplace without creativity. A workplace I can't afford, even if it is more comfortable for some people.

In the classic definition, management is getting results through people. Implicit in that definition is recognition that people will not get the desired results without management.

Implicit also in the definition is that the manager must get results through people as they are and not as the manager would like them to be. The challenge is getting people to *do* what must be done, not getting them to *be* a certain way. This means accepting all the differences and what those differences inevitably produce: conflict.

Managing conflict breaks into two parts: managing your own conflict with your colleagues and peers and managing conflict between your employees.

The first part is as important as the second, but many managers don't often consider that they must manage their own conflict.

I attend to my conflicts, however, in order to be more effective in achieving cooperation with other groups and departments and in order to set an example for employees in how to manage their conflicts.

What must be determined in any situation is whether the conflict is a matter of principle or a matter of territory. And the combinations are many, as I may be in conflict over principle and the other person may consider it a matter of territory. Or vice versa.

If my conflict is a matter of principle, I work toward compromise and consensus and avoid confrontation. If my conflict is a matter of protecting my territory, I just give in.

"Oh no," you're saying. "Nobody just gives in. Everybody protects his territory."

Wrong. I just give in. Turfiness is one of the more destructive forces in companies, and is never—repeat, never—worth the time and effort it consumes. Just as I know who the boss is without checking the parking assignments, I know what I'm responsible for without reading my job description.

If someone wants to take on an area of endeavor that I think I'm responsible for, I do not make an issue of it. Though I am good and I have consummate faith in my people, I might just learn something in the process of another manager or group doing something in "my" territory.

While I am not so sanguine in managing my conflicts that involve matters of principle, I do rely on a basic philosophy and one useful question.

The philosophy has to do with my belief in the presumption of goodwill. I try never to assume, no matter how hostile or aggressive the other person may be, that there is ill will between us. But listen, I'm not Saint Jim. It's not always easy to stay cool, and sometimes my sharp tongue gets unsheathed.

But I *always* regret it, and it is *always* counterproductive in the long run.

The useful question is a simple technique I learned a long time ago and have used many times. It never fails. When the disagreement or conflict reaches a point that seems an impasse, I ask, "What would you like me to do?"

The first reaction is astonishment. Then I elaborate, "If I could do anything to make this situation okay in your eyes, what would that be?"

You'd be surprised how often the desired action is something very simple and very easy to do. And you'd be surprised how often the other person just wants you to understand his or her viewpoint, not to change yours.

When there is an impasse, the *only* acceptable action is to agree to disagree and to keep talking. Avoid extreme positions. Think of the quote: "All extremes have one thing in common: they are rooted in stupidity."

And don't ask the boss to intervene. Taking your conflict to the boss is a failure of the worst sort. What it says is that you are not capable of dealing with your conflicts. It's like asking the boss to take over one of your job responsibilities.

Which leads to managing the conflict between your employees. A natural reaction of people in conflict is to find an authority figure to resolve things for them. We learned this easy way out when we were kids. Someone always seemed willing to sit in judgment.

Sitting in judgment is, in itself, a bit of a power trip, and you should not let employees suck you into the stern-judge position. Too many managers give in to that.

Get this: A lot of good managers have taken the bum rap of being called "indecisive" because they won't play stern judge. Often, when an employee complains that "I can't get the boss to make a decision," he's really saying, "I can't get things decided the way I want them decided."

Remember that, while you should not resolve the conflict through fiat, you are responsible to make it become an experience of growth and learning, despite who's *right*, rather than an experience of hostility and failure.

Another predictable reaction of people in conflict is to become angry and hostile. Most business cultures unwittingly encourage this through constant use of war and sports metaphors. Competition is consistently portrayed as battle. No one should be surprised then that disagreements among peers escalate into hostile, angry battles complete with subtle tactics and the recruiting of allies. It wastes time, energy, and talent.

Most conflicts should be decided through a process of talking honestly about the issues. Your role as manager is to bring about those conversations and to be a part of those conversations, as an advocate for *both* viewpoints (or however many there are). You must sit in the hot spot and ask the questions that bring the real issues to the table. Most of the conflict will be a clash of styles or personalities, so your job is to get to the heart of the disagreement, which, most likely, will be its substance.

I once was involved in the merger of two national organizations. There was so much history of conflict between these two groups that no one involved thought they ever would be merged.

I presided at many meetings, asking questions of representatives of both sides, trying to determine the issues. What I heard at first was a lot of operational blather, disagreements about how this or that function would be performed in the merged organization. Believe me, people never get really worked up over what the letterhead is going to look like or how the mail will be opened or how the offices will be laid out. What they get worked up over is where *their* name will appear on the letterhead, when they get *their* mail, and whether *their* office will be as nice as the next person's.

After many meetings, what finally revealed itself was that there were *no* issues of substance blocking the merger. Everything was style and procedural detail, arising out of perceived personal vulnerabilities. I asked for a volunteer committee made up of representatives of both organizations to work out all the details, with the understanding that the committee's work would be binding on all parties. No, the final agreement did not make everyone happy, but all the people who were focused on the overall goals of the resulting organization accepted it well. Furthermore, the process was a learning experience for everyone involved. It taught us that if there is a goal important enough, people can let go of their egos long enough to get it accomplished.

The real objective of resolving conflict, in fact, is that there are no winners or losers, just those who grew and learned and those who still need to go through the process a few times.

There may be situations in which conflict is so integral to the work that a more environmental—and less case-by-case —approach is appropriate.

The magazine business is full of such small daily conflicts, particularly between the editorial and design departments, the "word" people and the "art" people. Because these disagreements involve an aesthetic concern and affect work that is the creative output of a writer or designer, the conflict regularly becomes intense.

When I was editor in chief, I fell victim many times to the stern-judge trap. I tried to find a middle road, or I tried to make aesthetic judgments I was empowered to make but was not necessarily qualified to make. Of course my decisions didn't make the combatants happy, and no one learned anything from the process.

It became clear that the creative conflicts were unique in that they always involved matters of aesthetic judgment and rarely had to do with marketplace strategies or organizational changes or any kind of company policy or procedure.

What I needed was a change in the way the editors and designers regarded one another. I knew I could not make people care about one another, but I knew I could set up the conditions for people at least to get to know one another on a human level.

So I budgeted for a conference every year. We scheduled the meetings during the winter and met in nice, sunny places. We brought in outside speakers who addressed subjects of major social concern as well as the specific interests of editors and designers. And I encouraged celebrations of all sorts throughout the year.

I never expected the conflicts to disappear, and they didn't, but I did expect the intense *personal* hostility to subside, and it did. And I got out of the stern-judge business.

But by this time you're wondering, "What about the nasty conflicts, those really messy fights the manager finally has to do something about?"

Well, yes. There are those, and they are no fun. But they don't really come under the category of "managing conflict." That's not a cop-out though, because I do have a couple of thoughts on the subject of personal fights.

They happen probably more often in a creative group than any other. Sparks sometimes fly, and while it is best to treat those spats with benign neglect, they can become so disruptive you must do something.

The truth is, I've had to resort to some kind of scolding-father routine only about half a dozen times in thirty years. A good conversation, with me in the moderating role, works most of the time. But this technique can be *very* demanding.

In one case, I actually had to direct a conversation between two employees who had numerous behind-the-back complaints about one another. I took them to a meeting room in a neutral location; I said, "Let's proceed with goodwill, but I'm going to make you be honest."

I started the conversation by saying, "I hear that you, T——
——, have said that W———has poor work habits and that he abuses our tolerant environment. And I hear that you, W——
——, think that T———is a stiff-necked so-and-so. Either of you have a response?"

By purposely focusing on the most negative things I had heard, then overstating them somewhat, I gave both parties the chance to moderate the statement.

"No," they said individually, "I didn't say that; I said . . . etc."

So both were able to deny saying such a negative thing and, at the same time, to put on the table exactly what they did say.

From that point, I became a traffic director and *provocateur.*

Sometimes I said, "Stop. Let's get T———to respond to the points you've made before you go further."

The conversation required three hours. At the end, their relationship was on a new basis, with promises of honesty and straightforward confrontation, rather than backbiting. I was exhausted.

The objective was not to get them to love one another, only to care about one another within the context of their work lives.

I have employees today who will testify to the efficacy of this technique.

Managing conflict is never easy, but you must face the job head-on, because conflict and disagreement are predictable parts of the work process, particularly among people who work hard and care about what they do.

And I believe that conflict is simply part of the human condition, and that there cannot be good work without it. A good manager understands this and understands how to manage it—and would have it no different.

Managing Sameness: If It Ain't Broke, Break It!

I F YOU think managing conflict and managing diversity are loaded with problems, then you haven't thought through the problems of managing sameness. I'd far rather be faced with trying to achieve harmony and goodwill among people who are at one another's throats than try to squeeze an ounce of innovation or creativity or risk out of a company full of photocopies of one another.

One of the toughest management problems I ever had involved taking over a department in which the social architecture had been established years before and was thoroughly inculcated into everyone who joined the department. Almost like passing along the tribal myths.

This group did everything alike, from their dress to their social pastimes. Once a person was part of the group, he or she was part of the club. While the group produced competent work, there were people within the group who lacked competence but were protected by sort of a family blood attitude that fended off any outside inquiry about individual accomplishments.

Having read this far in this book, you know that I believe

in the work group as a community or family and that I believe the greater justice of the group often must transcend individual concerns.

But everything has extremes, and in this case the group ethic had gone too far. It had wiped out any one person's opportunity to excel, and individual effort beyond the norm was unacceptable. It was considered to be grandstanding or brownnosing.

From the company's viewpoint, the department was producing work that was beyond reproach, beyond harsh criticism, and until I took over, beyond serious question. I was already aware of the department and its work when the job was handed to me, so I adopted the attitude with the department's management that the work was *merely competent*.

Pause a minute and think about the problem. Here is a group of people who have no easily discernible shortcomings. If change is desired, what in the world does the manager say? "Hey, you people seem to be getting along very well. You smile. You never have conflict. Your work is okay. Things perk along on schedule, and the product sells okay. Sorry, we need a change." Sounds awkward if not downright silly.

The only thing to do in that situation is ask a lot of questions, focusing on the assumption that if things are okay with little apparent effort, could they be a lot better with more effort? Also, if we've been doing things the same way for a long time, how are we to know there's not a more effective way? I must have asked about research and direct customer contact a thousand times. The department's assumption had been that if the product was selling steadily, then there was no reason to question anything. You know—if it ain't broke, don't fix it.

Unfortunately, in today's business climate, by the time we wait for it to break, it's too late to fix it. I have a wise friend in the magazine business, John Mack Carter, who once said in a speech, "If it ain't broke, break it."

And there are a lot of constructive ways to "break" things. They begin with questioning the status quo and the conventional wisdoms.

A large customer service department of a mail-order fulfillment house offers a case in point. This operation consisted of people opening mail, writing letters, answering phones, all serving customer orders and dealing with complaints.

Most of these operations are very systems-driven, and this one was no exception. The work can get very dreary, but efficiency and productivity are the keys to profit.

Unlike the department I took over, these workers were very unhappy—but the managers had their systems working and could see no problem.

A new top manager was brought in. Early on, he met with the whole group and, against the advice of his managers, said, "I bet some of you really dislike these jobs."

The people were stunned. He continued, "And I bet some of you have great ideas for making things better without losing productivity. I want to hear the ideas."

He waited. The people were slow to start. Then the ideas came, and the mood change in the room was palpable. In *one* meeting, he "broke" the culture of that group in that he cracked the notion that the systems were worth more than the people, and he discarded the belief that "standardization" and "routine" and "procedure"—all aspects of the drive for sameness —were as important as responsive, happy people. In this case, he had to break things at the bottom in order to drag the managers into a spirit of innovation.

As for the department I took over, the changes I felt were needed took a while. They too required a change of management, a reorganization, and some forced growth, but the people finally began to let go of "how things are done" and began to look at how things might be done differently and better. Because the people were competent, for the most part, it stood to reason that some of them knew how things could be done better. The new management simply empowered them to come forward with those ideas.

Within a few years, things had changed drastically. There were new ideas. There was growth and, with the growth, opportunity for promotion and for bringing in new people.

The new department manager brought in people who did not necessarily fit the old mold. This only allowed more new ideas and more growth.

And what was most rewarding of all, the group ethic that simply had been an imposed sameness became a vibrant community of effort in which people supported one another out of enthusiasm and excitement and not out of obligation.

But there need be no drastic change in management to break a department of chronic sameness. You can do it in your own operation. The principles are as old as the hills. People need change. In business, the change normally should be evolutionary, not revolutionary, but when people or groups have stopped evolving, then the revolution may be called for. *Drastic change can be better than no change.*

People need growth, and when there is no change, there is no growth.

People need opportunity to achieve their own standards of excellence, and when there is no growth, there is no opportunity.

People need the sense of worth and well-being that comes from accomplishment and only from accomplishment, and when there is no opportunity, there is no accomplishment.

Without the sense of individual accomplishment, people will fall into a deadening sense of sameness, and the group standard will begin to decline to the level of the lowest common denominator.

This is not rare, and as I pointed out above, a group in this condition can produce merely competent work for quite a while. But if you as a manager don't recognize sameness for what it is and move to change it, the work will decline, and the group eventually will sink of its own dead weight.

If you are the manager who does not act in time to bring about change, you'll go down also.

PART V

RANDOM OBSERVATIONS AFTER TWENTY-EIGHT YEARS OF MANAGING

Random Observations After Twenty-eight Years of Managing

THERE'S AN old saw about management that gets a lot of us off on the wrong foot. It says that if all the employees did their jobs well, there would be no need for managers.

I've heard it, and you've heard it. And for many years, I accepted it without stopping to think about what it was saying and how it was forcing me to behave.

If my job as manager depends on at least some employees not doing their jobs well enough, then you can be damned sure I'll find employees who aren't doing their jobs well enough. And you can be sure I won't be putting my efforts into creating an environment in which people can do a good job better. Which, of course, is the real job of management.

A work group, whether you call it an accounting department or an editorial staff or a sales group or an orchestra, cannot operate as a collection of people who simply do their jobs well. To believe that is to disbelieve the power of the group to become more than the sum of its separate parts.

And to believe that the manager's job is only to assure that people do their jobs well is to return the manager to the old role of overseer or supervisor.

Staying Balanced

I know managers who cannot stay away from the office; it is as if they become insecure if they are not working. I'm not talking about those times we all have when things pile up and we have to take a Sunday and wade through the stack. I know people who come to the office when there are only the most routine things to deal with.

I also know managers who come in, read *The Wall Street Journal* and *The New York Times*, make some phone calls, dictate a few letters, have lunch with a crony, spend another couple of hours at the desk, leave in time for the 5:11 train, and think they've done a full day's work.

Neither work style says anything about commitment; the workaholic is no more committed than the lazy worker. Commitment has more to do with the quality of effort than with the number of hours in the office.

The balanced life lies somewhere in the middle, as it always does, and the middle changes from time to time, depending on the work load or perhaps the newness of the job.

Finding the middle is the tough part, but you have to keep at it. Otherwise you'll find yourself one day without resources.

Even workaholics retire. Sooner or later, they will lose the job that so preoccupies them. Then what?

At the other end of the spectrum are those who may lose the job because they are so preoccupied with everything but the job. Then what?

My advice for finding the middle is very simple. Consider everything of equal importance: job, family, friends, church, clubs, volunteer work, exercise, sports, hobbies, and killing time.

Walk the balance board and make time for it all. Otherwise you'll face that inevitable moment of truth when you'll wonder where the hell all the time went.

Chief Cheerleader

ʾout twenty years ago, I became manager of a department
ʾle who were overworked, underpaid, and generally

demoralized. Nonetheless, they worked hard and produced good work despite their problems. But it was only a matter of time before we would face heavy turnover and a debilitating disruption of work.

It was one of the happiest experiences of my career. I had but to take off the harnesses and let them run. We brought their salaries up to date. Then I made time each day to reassure every person that mistakes were okay and I was not waiting to beat on them.

One day, one of the senior people asked, "You know what some of the people are calling you around here?

"No," I said. "Should I want to know?"

"It's not bad. They're saying you are the chief cheerleader."

Not bad indeed, I thought. In fact, I later told my boss that I thought of that label as part of my job description.

After not many more years in management, I began to think of "chief cheerleader" as part of every good manager's job description.

DRAWING THE LINE ON MISTAKES

It is important to make mistakes, and it is important to let your employees make mistakes. It is so important, in fact, that most of the popular management books of the past few years have made a big subject of it.

What few seem to address, however, is when to stop a mistake before it gets made.

It is given that a good manager frequently sees an employee headed for a mistake well before the critical point comes. So when should the manager act to avoid the mistake?

I think of this problem as a flight instructor. It is also important to let student pilots make mistakes. Obviously, though, the instructor can't permit the student to crash and burn, so he waits until that critical point at which the student realizes the mistake but at which the airplane can still be controlled. *And he never permits the mistake that can be made only once.*

Not a bad guide for managers. As long as people can learn

from mistakes, encourage risk-taking. But do not allow any mistake that threatens the operation's survival.

SHARING OWNERSHIP

How many times have you read about this in the past few years? Plenty. Some CEO is always saying, "We get everyone to buy into the vision; we try to instill our employees with a sense of ownership."

Sense of ownership, hell! How about some real ownership? I think the subject of ownership deserves more examination by management as well as by the employees. There are plenty of examples that employee-owned businesses can create real advantages for themselves. How, then, can some kind of employee ownership be accommodated within the context of a publicly owned corporation or a large private corporation?

But ownership, as we know, is not just a matter of dividing up the rewards. How also can the problems and responsibilities of ownership be shared and felt?

Share it all, I say. Adjust the compensation systems so that employees get a piece of the business. Institute performance-based bonuses. Include stock awards throughout the lifetime of a career. Let employees feel the pride of knowing they are building the longtime welfare of themselves and their families.

But let them also feel the frustration of rising medical and other benefit costs, escalating taxes, shortages of resources and materials, price pressures, share struggles, and increasing global competition.

I think the full experience of shared ownership—the pain as well as the joy of it—can hold more potential for the reinvigoration of a business than any other single factor.

DECISIONS, DECISIONS

If ever a manager can say, with absolute certainty, *I* made that decision, then something is wrong with the operation.

The day of the single decision-maker is gone, if ever it existed. Even the entrepreneurs who so pride themselves on being one-man bands realize at some point that their businesses will be limited by their unwillingness to let other imaginations and judgment get into the act.

ONE MORE THOUGHT ABOUT FIRING

No one ever believes he or she is justly fired. There must be some sort of immune system that protects us from facing the reality of our own failures.

So what can a manager do but try to determine what he or she wants that fired employee to come away with? What understandings? What lessons? And what hopes?

I want people I've fired to know why and to decide for themselves what might have been done. I want them to learn what to do next time. And I want them to realize that they still have a future, and they will grow enormously in embracing that future.

But I don't expect ever to convince anyone of that, and when indeed a person I've fired does learn and grow and make a better life, I don't expect to be thanked.

Nonetheless, I have the satisfaction of knowing that only one or two people did not go on to better things after I fired them. The rest of them have done well.

The nagging question, of course, is if they've done well somewhere else, why didn't they do well for me?

It's a question that can keep me awake nights.

THE BELL CURVE IS FOR DUMBBELLS

Dumbbell managers, that is. And there are still plenty of them who believe that, in a perfect world, worker performance will be distributed on a bell curve throughout the work force.

What nonsense. On the one hand, we speak the glowing phrases. We talk about motivating people to rise above themselves, about creating environments for quality work, about building a passion for excellence. Then, when we want to set up appraisal and compensation systems, we cannot accept that perhaps—*just perhaps*—we've been so successful as managers that there is no bell curve, that the distribution of performance and abilities is distorted toward excellence.

The bell curve is management for statisticians, not performers.

MANAGING AS PARENTING

A touchy subject, this, but one that every manager comes to understand at some point in the career.

Part of the touchiness comes from the old paradigm of the boss-as-father with his paternalistic indulgence on one side and harsh judgment and disapproval on the other. This has become the symbol of bad management, and for good reason.

But there is another way to look at manager as parent. Patricia Pollock, managing editor of a custom publishing department at the Meredith Corporation, wrote, as part of a guest editorial for the company's management newsletter, "I've also learned a lot from raising children. I spent a lot of time with the kids trying to solve all their problems for them, and along the way I realized that this was not what I was supposed to do. I learned to create an atmosphere so they could learn how to cope with a problem and solve it themselves.

"In the same way, as a manager, I don't believe in being the provider of answers—people need to learn on their own. This turns out to be trusting people."

What a perfect expression of the manager as parent. And it is appropriate that a woman manager wrote it. Few men managers would be that open, that guileless, and that willing to be credited (or blamed) with such a thought in print.

Yet I hear many managers express these parallel concerns about kids and employees: how to pay attention and lead and teach without doing too much for them; how to encourage individual risk-taking while making sure they don't go too far; how to reward and recognize the accomplishments of one while still caring about another who does not do as well.

As a "parent" in the workplace, the manager must give daily expressions of pride and satisfaction in both the professional and the personal accomplishments of employees.

And those expressions must be sincere. You can't fake it. Part of a loving and caring environment happens because of the manager's commitment to grow from a genuine interest in, and concern for, the growth of his or her employees.

Exactly the same is true of parents.

THE MYTH OF BEING OVERQUALIFIED

I've never turned down any job applicant because I felt he or she was overqualified, and I wonder about managers who do.

The "overqualified" label means one of three things:

1. The manager is afraid that the applicant has been around so long that he or she has a lot of bad habits, but the manager won't make the effort to find out.

2. The manager is intimidated by the applicant's qualifications and feels threatened or not qualified to manage him or her.

3. The manager is playing God and deciding whether the applicant will be happy in the job or not.

I don't believe that any good manager, with five minutes' reflection, could make a case against hiring the most qualified person possible in every job, whatever its level.

The only issue should lie with the applicant: Does the person understand fully the limitations as well as the responsibilities of the job? If so, I say let 'em at it.

COMMUNION OF THE SAINTS

In the oldtime religion of my youth, we believed that through the ritual of what we called "the Lord's Supper," we communed with the saints, with all those who had gone before.

I was struck with this old image at a retirement dinner as the retiree invoked the names of company people long dead and spoke of them as if they were just on some kind of sabbatical. He talked of what they had taught the people who had taught him, and how he had tried to teach others who were now teaching the beginners.

As he spoke, we realized that a true community has no limit in time. He made us feel the extension of our community of work, into a time long before us and into a time yet to come.

As if the work exists in and of itself, and we come and go from it in a kind of continuum of endeavor, in a kind of communion.

GOOD NEWS/BAD NEWS

There was a time when I had great doubts about my abilities and about my career. It was a time of personal trauma and a huge job change.

A close friend sent me a letter with a single sentence.

I now share it with every employee or colleague who's suffering from a lapse of self-confidence. One of these days, I plan to get a calligrapher to do it up right, then I'll frame it and hang in on the wall of whoever needs it at the time:

THE ORIGINAL GOOD NEWS/BAD NEWS:
YOU ARE AS GOOD AS YOU WERE AFRAID YOU ARE.

JUDGING WHAT'S IMPORTANT

I'm always getting surprised by the gap between my perception of the importance of an act and the perception of the other person involved.

A few weeks ago, I had dinner with a colleague, a person who reports to me. The dinner was squeezed into a busy travel schedule, but there had been a recent death in his family, and I felt somehow moved to make the time.

The dinner was pleasant though unremarkable, yet in a few days I received a letter of profuse gratitude for my having taken the time. I was stunned and a bit ashamed for not having imbued the evening with nearly the importance my colleague gave it.

On another occasion, I turned on my computer to find an updated word-processing program installed. I was irritated because, having only a few years ago given up my old manual typewriter, I was just getting used to the old program. I was peevish about the change, and asked that the old program be reinstalled.

Only later, after the damage was done, did I realize that the programmer who installed the new software surely was very hurt. She had worked hard to get the new program in while I was on a trip, thinking I would be delighted by it. Far from being thanked for the effort, she had to do double work.

I could have kicked myself.

We managers just have to realize that what is important to the employees is what the employees think is important, and we have to measure our impact on those matters. Too often we forget that our words and actions carry weight out of all proportion with the import we may have intended.

VOLUNTEER AND LEARN

If as a manager you think it is difficult to get results through people over whom you have some authority, imagine how it is to get results through people *without any authority over them whatsoever*.

That's the description of volunteer work.

There is no better place to learn the subtle points of management than as an officer of a volunteer organization, be it a volunteer health agency or the board of an educational institution or the Boy Scouts or the PTA.

I have heard people describe these jobs as "thankless" and without reward.

Not true. Most of them are involved with doing good and doing good work, reward enough in itself, and the people I know who volunteer regularly are richly rewarded.

Beyond the spiritual reward is a management learning experience beyond anything they could dream up in business school.

As a member of, and then president of, the board of directors of a national voluntary health agency, I was involved in a near-bankruptcy situation, a complete reorganization, the hiring of new staff, restructuring the board, redoing the fundraising apparatus, introducing a new planning process, lobbying for congressional action, leading national conferences, and participating in the successful merger of two national organizations.

All that was accomplished without benefit of *authority*. All of us on the board were driven only by our concern for the cause to seek consensus and workable solutions for every nasty problem.

I learned about influence and quiet persuasion, about good committee work, about getting the best possible work from people who were sincere and well-intended but not very qualified for the tasks for which they had volunteered. (You can't "fire" an incompetent volunteer.)

This experience has served me countless times in my business life.

I encourage all my managers to find a cause, to volunteer, to learn, and to grow. There are no failures in volunteer work.

THE INTERNAL JOB DESCRIPTION

People do well what they want to do, and they do not do well what they do not want to do.

It's as true of managers as of anyone.

So do a check once in a while to make sure your job description on paper matches the one in your heart.

If not, it's time to change the one on paper.

THE WILLINGNESS TO CARE

There's a problem with creating what I call the loving and caring workplace, and it is that no one person can love and care for all the employees all the time. The daily act of caring is very hard work.

So you have to choose other managers who have the willingness to care. You have to focus on nurturing your good, close managers, then teach them to pass it along.

Spread the caring, spread the work.

EMPTY THREATS

Remember this: People who consistently threaten to leave do not want to leave. They want you to ask them to stay. They need to hear that you care about them and that they are valuable in your eyes.

One of the young managers in my group came to me about a good creative person who, every six months or so, threatened to leave.

"What are the issues?" I asked. "Pay?"

"No," the manager said, "that's what makes it so damned frustrating. He doesn't demand anything; he just says this place is getting to him and he's going to quit."

"So what have you told him?"

"I've been telling him that this is a good place to work and that he won't do better anywhere else, but if he has decided to leave, that's his decision."

"And he stays."

"Yes, but next time, I'm going to tell him I'm tired of being threatened and he should just leave."

Well, yes. That is the temptation, I admit, because I've felt the same way.

But I said, "Lighten up and try this. Just look him in the eye and say, 'Look, I really want you to stay. Your work is very good, and you are a valuable part of this department. I've been worried that you're going to leave, so I'm asking you to tell me you're going to stay so I can stop worrying.' "

"But that's like begging!" the manager said, red in the face.

"So," I said, "is it so bad if it solves the problem?"

Not only did my advice work, but it changed their relationship and changed the atmosphere in the department.

OLD-FASHIONED EMPLOYEE

I once heard a speaker make the point that 90 percent of the men of my generation profess to want an "old-fashioned wife."

He asked for a show of hands. "How many of you men

would say 'Aren't I lucky' if you had a wife who says she loves you so much she wants to satisfy you completely and sacrifice her own ambitions and just let you grow and develop?"

With some laughing and some overstatement, I suspect, there were a lot of hands in the air.

Then the speaker asked, "How many of you would accept that same kind of love from your children?"

There were no hands. And the point was made that one cannot sacrifice one's own growth and call it love. Conversely, it is not love to accept another's sacrifice of growth, because love is about growth.

Which begs the question about the self-sacrificing, ever-loyal, do-anything-for-the-company employee.

Yes, I believe in loyalty. Yes, I believe in love in the work-place. Yes, I believe there are times when we must give beyond ourselves for the good of the group and the achievement of the goal.

But it is not giving of one's best self to be constantly sacrificing one's own opportunities for "the good of the company" or out of loyalty to the boss.

And it is *terrible* management to either demand or accept an employee's sacrifice of advancement or opportunity or growth and call it "loyalty" to the manager.

Think about it this way: You wouldn't accept that from your children.

THE BAG OF TRICKS

Face it. We have our bag of tricks. All managers do, and those tricks can be both valuable and limiting.

A lot of managers think themselves lucky to have changed jobs just as they had done all the obvious things they knew to do.

The luckier managers, by far, are those who had to stay with a job after the bag of tricks was empty and who had to start inventing the job fresh every day.

Then, and only then, the growing begins.

A NOTE ABOUT GREED

One of my early lessons in business was taught to me by a man who thought he was doing me a favor.

"The marketplace is driven by greed," he said. "Take it or leave it, that's the way business is."

Unfortunately, I bought into that statement for a long time before I realized that, like many simple statements, it requires a lot of definition.

By greed, did my mentor mean self-interest or selfishness? If indeed the marketplace is driven by the greed of selfishness, then the marketplace by its nature is hard on the human spirit. It is all the things its critics say it is.

If on the other hand the marketplace is driven by an enlightened self-interest in which our self-interest is served as we serve others, then it can help ennoble the human spirit.

If the marketplace is hard on the human spirit, how has it survived in the world of humans?

Or could it be that those who believe in the greed of the marketplace have just found a convenient excuse for their own greed or for their own unwillingness to concern themselves with the human spirit? Maybe they hide their self-serving ambitions, their willingness to do harm, their disregard for humanity in the workplace, and their harsh management techniques behind the more abstract concept of the "marketplace."

I do not doubt the presence of greed in the marketplace, because I do not doubt the presence of greed in people.

But I also do not doubt the ennobling aspects of work, of the workplace, of the community of endeavor, of the marketplace.

So I choose to believe that most of the marketplace is driven by people who want to do good work for others and for themselves.

The Manager's Little Piece of Immortality

A FEW weeks ago, I received an invitation to a reunion of the 48th Tactical Fighter Wing that was based in Chaumont, France, from the early 1950s until 1959. The invitation was specific: It was not for all former 48th people, just those who had served in Chaumont.

I left the air force in 1959, and much has happened in my life since then. Why, I wondered, would I be so tempted to join this group of people, most of whom I no longer know? What would we have in common? What could we talk about?

Days in Chaumont, of course. Flying. Partying. Cutting the tie off the new wing commander his first night in the club. Mock dogfights with the French out of Saint-Dizier. Bombing on the range in Libya. Flying low over the rivers and canals and vineyards of Burgundy. Crashes. Death.

Nothing special as military experiences go, except to the extent that the intensity of the experience itself made it special. And except to the extent of being isolated in Chaumont, where the living was fairly primitive, made it special. And except to the extent that our bonds as members of a community made it special.

Every year, former military people gather for reunions of their old units, many of them from World War II, meeting once again after forty-five or fifty years to relive times made special by the intensity of an experience.

If nothing else, it is proof that the most lasting friendships, the most enduring memories, are those born of intense relationships in a community of mutual endeavor, temporary though it may be.

A few months before receiving the invitation to the 48th reunion, I attended a retirement dinner for a colleague who had been with our company for thirty-five years or so and with whom I had worked for twenty of those years.

In but a few minutes, she recalled the years, telling anecdote after anecdote, the silly stuff, the complaints, the jokes, the hard work. She reminisced about people now retired or dead and told how they had shaped her life and career. Each department she had worked in became its own experience within those thirty-five years. It was clear that she did not think of the years as a whole, or remember them as one continuing jumble of professional experience.

It was as if her career were divided into eras.

Not long after that dinner, I attended a sales conference at which a retiring senior manager was honored.

He spoke eloquently, and his themes were the same. He told us the stories that have become part of our corporate mythology, even as he was recognizing, and taking, his place in that mythology.

His final remarks were for the young people, the sellers now out there doing the everyday hard stuff. He told them he knew the world is different now, but he asked them not to think of it as all that different, because, he said, the important things endure: honesty, integrity, hard work, service, courage.

Then he asked those young people to look to all the good salespeople who had gone before, those he had cited as influencing his life. "You'll never know them," he said, "and I'm sorry you won't, but I've tried to teach you what they taught me."

I thought, of course they *do* know those people whom they never met. They know them through you.

Within another few weeks, there came a third retirement party, this time for a personnel director, a man I never thought of as being particularly good with words and until then would never have described as eloquent.

Among his comments were these: "I have worked the last twenty-two years for a company that cares about people and expresses that concern by action. I have been a part of that, so I know what *success* is. . . .

"I have not fulfilled all my objectives, my hopes, my dreams, so I know what *adjustment* is. . . .

"And because I have known all these things, I truly know *contentment*."

It would be easy to write off these reminiscences as simple sentimentality. After all, it's pretty easy to be abiding and loving about most any experience when you're leaving it forever. Even prisoners have expressed nostalgia for the penitentiary.

It would be easy also to say that business has changed: Almost no one these days expects to stay with a company for decades and then retire.

But to ignore what these retirees said is to ignore a major lesson for management. The lesson has to do with recognizing that our careers, like our lives, somehow divide themselves into eras, into distinct periods involving distinct kinds of experiences. People come and go and are identified with these periods. And the success of the enterprise frequently rides on the ability of the people to create a community of effort within each era.

At the center of it is the manager. One way or another, the manager will become part of the mythology. He or she has the opportunity to create an environment in which the experience of mutual enterprise is so intense that the people who participated in that time and that place want to recall it forever. Whether those people stuck around the company until retirement or moved on to another company is irrelevant to the intensity and the memorability of the experience.

Think of the eras of your own life. They could include school years and the first job and, as in my life, an intense military experience. Never mind that all the people who served at Chaumont in the fifties went on to other lives, other experiences, some of which were just as intense and binding. The point is that those years are set in our memories for all time, transcending whatever happened before or after. Nothing can change it, and nothing can take it away.

Those same kinds of experiences and feelings happen in business day after day and year after year, more than any outside observer would ever guess. And when they happen, the manager's place in the shared history is passed along for generations, as each person who lived through those eras retires and makes the speech we all hope to get to make someday.

What more could a leader/manager/mentor/coach/friend ask for in this world? It's as close to immortality as a businessperson ever gets.